THE WEST MIDLANDS METRO

AND VERY LIGHT RAIL

By David Voice

Published by Adam Gordon

ALSO BY DAVID VOICE

How to Go Tram and Tramway Modelling
London's Tramways Their History and How to Model Them
What Colour Was That Tram?
Tramway Modelling in 'OO' Gauge
More Tramway Modelling in 'OO' Gauge
The Illustrated History of Kidderminster and Stourport Electric Tramway (with Melvyn Thompson)
How to Go Tram and Tramway Modelling, 2nd Edition
The Millennium Guide to Trams in the British Isles
The Definitive Guide to Trams in the British Isles
Toy and Model Trams of the World, Volume 1 and Volume 2: with Gottfried Kuře
Next Stop Seaton! (with David Jay), editions 1-3
How to Go Tram and Tramway Modelling, 3rd edition
Hospital Tramways and Railways, 1st and 2nd editions
Freight on Street Tramways in the British Isles
British Tramcar Manufacturers, British Westinghouse and Metropolitan-Vickers
Works Tramcars of the British Isles
The Age of the Horse Tram
Monorails of the World
Tram and Bus Tokens of the British Isles
Battery Trams of the British Isles
Mono-Rail, The History of the industrial monorails made by Road Machines Ltd, Metalair Ltd, and Rail Machines Ltd
Tramway Reflections
Shocking Solutions to a Current Problem
Seaton Tramway—Its Electric
Seaton Tramway—The Valentine's Day Storm
The History of Worcester's Tramways
Last Rides—Funeral Trams Around the World
All Dressed Up and Somewhere to Go, the History of Decorated Tramcars in the British Isles
Slot Machines, The History of Cable Hauled Street Tramways in the British Isles
Kidderminster and Stourport Electric Tramway Company Ltd.
Explosive Power on Tramways in the British Isles
Tramways of the Potteries
Next Stop Seaton 4rth Edition.
The Tramways of Brighton and the Surrounding Area.

The Author

David Voice has been interested in trams, both full size and model, for as long as he can remember. He is the author of many books about tramways and tram modelling; he has also been published extensively in the model railway press. David has recently retired as the Small Scale Modelling Adviser to the Tramway and Light Railway Society, a role he held for over 40 years.

Copyright: All rights to text and photographs (except where identified) are reserved to David Voice. Every care has been taken to ensure the accuracy of the information contained in this publication but no liability can be accepted for any errors or omissions.

A catalogue entry for this book is available from the British Library
ISBN 978-1-910654-32-3
Publication no. 136

Published in 2022 by Adam Gordon, Kintradwell Farmhouse, Brora, Sutherland KW9 6LU Tel: 01408 622660

Printed by 4edge, 22 Eldon Way Industrial Estate, Hockley, Essex, SS5 4AD.

Production by Barnabas Gordon

WEST MIDLANDS METRO
CONTENTS

Tramcar number 27 at the Centenary Square stop in January 2020. This was the westward terminus from November 2019 until the Broad Street extension opened in 2021. On the route from Grand Central Station the trams had no overhead and used battery power. Behind the tram is, on the left the International Convention Centre, on the right the Birmingham Repertory Theatre and out of the picture further right, the Central Library.

INTRODUCTION

Living in Kidderminster and working in Birmingham, and having a great interest in tramways, I naturally followed the progress of the Midland Metro in detail. My friend John Boynton was a notable historian of local railways and wrote the history of the Birmingham to Wolverhampton railway and its closure and subsequent conversion into the Midland Metro. His book "Main Line to Metro (Birmingham Snow Hill – Wolverhampton)" was published in 2001 and included the building and first two years of operation of the tramway. This and a book published in 2015 focusing on the Metro's T69 fleet of trams titled "An Illustrated History of the Midland Metro T69 Trams" by Andrew Coward told the early days of the system. Otherwise the West Midlands Metro (as it is now known) has not been the subject of any other book.

At the end of 2019 I thought that it was an appropriate time to review the history of the tramway and bring it up to date. Having made a start on researching my book the world woke up to the impact of an unusual virus called Covid 19. To begin with it made little difference to work on the book. But early in 2020 travel restrictions limited visiting the tramway. The impression given was that this would pass over in a couple of months. This lengthened to the whole of the year. 2021 did not start any better, with another lock down, the longest yet. From the start of the pandemic the income of public transport of all kinds suffered badly with trains and buses seeking emergency funding from the government to keep services running, albeit at reduced levels. Initially tramways were not included, until it was pointed out that they were a vital service getting employees to and from work particularly in essential areas such as health, police, and fire. National funds were allocated to keep the tramway services running. However, a totally unforeseen issue, faults in the tramcars, brought the system to a halt three times in nine months. Indeed, I agreed with my publisher that the book should be printed during the third closed period, as it was already two years behind schedule.

ACKNOWLEDGEMENTS

It would not have been possible to write this book without the very generous help I received from many people and organisations who have considerable knowledge of the system. In every case they have happily shared information and guided me to further resources. Without all this help the book would be smaller and less informative. I owe a great debt of gratitude to each and every one.

Roger Monk had followed the building of the Metro closely and recorded events with his camera. He very kindly allowed me full access to the photographs he took and information he had gathered. I have identified the photographs he has taken, which are a small selection of his whole collection. I am extremely grateful to him for his generosity.

The members of the Industrial Railway Society and contributors to the "On Track Plant" website have followed the history of the West Midlands Metro and have gathered detailed information about the construction and maintenance operations of the Metro and have generously shared their knowledge with me. In particular I would like to thank Kev Adlam and Roy Hennefer for allowing me to use photographs they have taken.

The Tramways and Urban Transport magazine proved a bountiful source of information both for the early discussions and proposals to build tramways in the West Midlands and for a commentary on the design, construction and operation of the system. Detailed information was published in the "NEWSHEADLINES" columns, the regular "Worldwide Review" and specific articles on the Metro. There were, and still are, many contributors to these articles and I thank them all and particularly the Home News Editor, John Symons. Other invaluable information was obtained from the British Trams Online and the West Midlands Metro websites and local newspapers. Google Earth gave the opportunity to see the system and its developments without leaving home. A great advantage during times of Coronavirus lockdown.

I also thank Alan Kirkman for all the help and invaluable information he has provided throughout my time as an author. When I am confronted by an insoluble problem I know that Alan will either give me the answer or will know who can.

I owe sincere thanks Adam and Barnabas Gordon for their invaluable advice and guidance for the many years that they have been publishing my books. I am indebted to them.

For the views and facts expressed in this book I am solely responsible. If any reader can supply additional information or corrections please contact me via the publisher.

Cars 06 and 15 of the original fleet seen at Wednesbury Parkway on 4 July 2014.

CHAPTER 1

Brief History of Earlier Tramways in Birmingham and Wolverhampton

Under a quirk in the Tramways Act of 1870 Local Authorities were allowed to lay tramways in their streets but were prohibited from running any trams on the lines. Instead only privately owned Companies could be given the powers to run a tram service. Initially the source of power was horses, but soon mechanical alternatives were being used. First came steam locomotives hauling large tram trailers. But this was not a satisfactory solution (particularly with mothers on washday when the soot and embers emitted by the locomotives spoiled washing drying on the line).

The first electrically operated tramway in the Metro area was a battery powered tram locomotive that was given a trial by the Birmingham Central Tramway in 1888. Using the Julien system and built by Elwell-Parker of Wolverhampton, the tram locomotive hauled a steam trailer along part of the Bournbrook line. The trial was a success and an order was placed for twelve accumulator, passenger carrying tramcars, numbers 101 - 112. The service started on 25 July 1890 and a further two battery cars were added in 1892. The Birmingham Central Tramways Company was taken over by the City of Birmingham Tramways Company in 1896 who, in 1901, persuaded the City Council to allow an overhead electric supply to be fitted. All the tramways in the city were acquired by the Corporation and a programme of electrifying the remaining horse tramway routes began in 1904.

The trial of the Juien battery locomotive that convinced the Birmingham Central Tramways to replace their steam tram engines with self contained battery tramcars. Photo TLRS Archive.

Birmingham Central tramcars in the battery exchange area of the depot. Depleted batteries were removed and replaced with newly recharged units.

Meanwhile the Manager of the South Staffordshire Tramways, Alfred Dickinson, had been exploring the use of an overhead wire system using tramcars with trolley poles. He patented a design for a trolley mast and pole. The proposal to convert to overhead electrical supply was approved by all the necessary Councils and the new overhead electrical supply opened to the public on 1 January 1893.

South Staffordshire Tramways tram number 40 outside the newly built power station.

The City of Birmingham Tramways Company introduced overhead powered electric tramcars on Birmingham tramways .

The British Electric Traction Company purchased the bankrupt Dudley and Wolverhampton Tramway Company's steam tramway with the intention to regauge the line to 3ft 6in and convert it to electric power. That part of the system that was within the Wolverhampton borough was sold to that Council. Both new owners set about converting the lines to electric operation. There was little agreement between the two, for example the Corporation decided on the Lorain Stud Contact system, while the Company decided to use the overhead wire system. The British Electric Traction Company renamed its part of the tramway the Wolverhampton District Electric Tramways Limited. The Corporation and Company lines through Bilston were opened to electric tramcars in 1902, though the two systems could not run on the other's track due to the different current collection systems.

Looking very much like a Sunday School boys outing, the absence of a trolley pole on Wolverhampton Corporation car 11 shows the power supply is by stud contact.

By 1904 the tramway legislation had changed and Corporations were permitted to operate tramways. As Birmingham Corporation owned all the track in the city their thoughts turned to running the tramways themselves. The legislation allowed Councils to purchase operating tramways at what was called "scrap" prices at the end of set periods. Birmingham took advantage of this and over the years gradually acquired the whole system. By 1912 the operation of all the lines in the city had been taken over by the Corporation. The city expanded and the Corporation Tramway took over more of the Company owned lines that were in those areas that were absorbed.

The staff pose for their photograph on this Wolverhampton District uncanopied tramcar.

In the 1920's and 1930's the changes in way people lived were influencing the tramways. The cost of staffing tramways had risen faster than inflation; the effect of the depression meant there was less demand for travel to and from work; while the affluent middle classes were enjoying the benefits of car ownership and started regarding the tramcar as an obstruction in the road. The numbers of passengers declined and it was the outbreak of the Second World War that gave a second chance to tramways. They did not rely on petrol from abroad, but could run on electricity generated using coal from British pits but there was a downside. Many tramway men responded to the call for volunteers for the forces and their replacements were new to the role.

Spare parts for tramcars were scarce and bombing raids on cities damaged many tramcars and track. In Coventry this led to the complete abandonment of the tramway. By the end of hostilities most British tramways were in a very sorry state and spares were still almost non-existent. The bus industry stepped in with the promise of brand new buses that were far cheaper than new trams and far more acceptable to the public than old trams. In Birmingham, the Corporation had experimented with trolleybus operation in the 1920's, which were cheaper than replacing worn track, overhead and tramcars. However, the trolley-bus routes had a relatively short life with the last one closing in July 1951, two years earlier than the aban-donment of the tramway. However, it was the diesel bus that gained most favour with local politicians. Seen as less expensive and more flexible than tramcars in a city that had a thriving automobile industry the future was inevitable. It was delayed by the War, but the tramcar succumbed to the inevitable.

The last tramcar ran on 4ᵗJuly 1953 and public transport in the city was limited to trains, buses and cabs. While a core of Birmingham residents continued to miss the trams, the Council promoted using buses for street public transport.

At this point it is helpful to examine the complexities of the structures of the organisations involved in the ownership, building and operation of the Midland Metro. Under the Transport Act 1968 implemented on 1 October 1969, the responsibility for the operation and coordination of public transport in large conurbations was vested in Public Transport Executives (PTE's). In the West Midlands the West Midlands PTE was given the responsibility for public passenger transport in its area. This was a vast area including the City of Birmingham, the County Boroughs of Dudley, Solihull, Walsall, Warley, West Bromwich and Wolverhampton, plus those parts of Staffordshire, Warwickshire and Worcestershire adjacent to the PTE area. It included all the public bus operations and railway services in the area. The PTE also had responsibility for any tramway services built in its area.

New in 1904 one of the smart Corporation tramcars, as befitted the second city in the land.

In 1970 there was an interesting development in Birmingham when the Royal Mail opened a tunnel be-tween their newly opened main sorting office in Navigation Street and New Street Railway Station. The 400m long tunnel ran under Seven Street to the station, joining existing tunnels connecting the station to Victoria Square sorting office. The tunnel had a level surface and battery tugs hauled wheeled cages of mail to and from the trains. It provided a secure link between the station and the sorting office, such that there was a rumour that dealers in precious stones in the Jewellery Quarter would post their most expensive gems to themselves on a Friday evening as it was cheaper than paying bank fees for hiring a secure strong box for weekend storage. However, the tunnel became redundant when the sorting office moved to new premises in Aston in 1998. The old sorting office was purchased by developers in 1999 and converted to restaurants, shops and offices. It reopened in its new guise in 2001.

There was another change in 1973, when, under the 1972 Local Government Act, the West Midlands Metropolitan County was created. This added Meriden and Coventry to its area (at one time it was possible that Bromsgrove and Redditch would be added to the West Midland PTE's responsibility, but the idea was abandoned). A major change in Birmingham was the transfer of Midland Red bus services (and the buses operated by them) to West Midlands PTE. Midland Red continued to serve routes in the Shire counties. The transferred buses were given a new livery from all over red to Birmingham deep blue and cream. This was applied directly over the existing red paint, which soon leeched through creating a new blue and and bright pink colour scheme.

Birmingham Corporation tramcars running at the junction at Carter's Green, West Bromwich. The Council owned the tramway in its Borough, but leased it to tramway operators. From 1902 to 1924 it was leased to South Staffordshire Tramways and Birmingham Corporation took over in 1924.

Summary of the early electric tramways between Birmingham and Wolverhampton

Bilston – Wolverhampton District Electric Tramways purchased the Bilston and District electric tramway in 1900 and added to the network. The section between Willenhall and Darlaston was taken over by the Walsall Corporation Tramways in 1925. The Wolverhampton District Tramways transferred the rest of the tramway to the Dudley, Stourbridge and District Electric Traction Company in 1928. The final lines closed in 1930.

Birmingham – Birmingham Corporation opened from 1904 with West Bromwich tramways being added in 1911. The Corporation tramways closed in 1953

Handsworth – The tramways were run by South Staffordshire Tramways from 1902 to 1911 then Birmingham Corporation until closure in 1953

Wednesbury – In 1902 the Borough Council compulsorily purchased the tramways in their area and then leased them back to the South Staffordshire Tramways Company. The situation was complicated by a boundary between Wednesbury and Darlaston Councils running down the middle of a tram route. After much argument, an agreement was reached that satisfied all the parties.

West Bromwich – The tramway was leased to South Staffordshire Tramways from 1902 to 1924 when the lease expired. The Council then approached Birmingham Corporation to reach an agreement where the routes were operated by Birmingham Tramways.

Wolverhampton – Wolverhampton Corporation Tramways operated from 1900 until closing in 1928.

This was resolved as each repainted vehicle came due for a scheduled repaint as a cream less prone to leeching was applied.

In 1979 the Birmingham Post reported that James Isaac, Director General of the PTE, commented that West Midlands commuters could be travelling to work by trams, trolleybuses and electric trains by the end of the century. The Council was to be asked to approve appointing consultants to advise on the use of electric traction as part of the County Structure Plan, due later in the year. This led to a joint Planning Committee being established in 1981 by the West Midlands County Council and the West Midlands Passenger Transport Executive to explore whether light rail was a solution to the city's public transport future. The PTE announced that County Councillors were being invited to visit Newcastle and a number of European cities with the view to exploring the feasibility of introducing a light rail network in their area. The PTE, County Council and British Rail announced in November that they were carrying out a survey to identify the likely number of passengers that would use a cross city link from Solihull to Stourbridge. In the following year, the County Council published their County Structure Plan Review that included proposals for a Rapid Transit system that could be developed before 1991. In April 1983 the County Council included a possible rapid transit System in its County Structure Plan Review. Then in June consultants were appointed to report by October on the feasibility of rapid transit in the area. In September 1983 the Council announced that a "guided busway" had been proposed and plans were being made for its construction. The scheme would consist of 700 metres of guided roadway laid on a central reservation and the purchase of fifteen specially adapted buses.

The reserved section of Tracline in the central reservation of Streetly Road.

The "guided busway" (called "Tracline 65") was opened on 9 October in Short Heath along the Streetly Road. This was the first in this country. Along a 600-metre length of a dual carriageway on route 65 a shallow trough was laid in the central reservation allowing adapted buses to manoeuvre along the route. The sides of the trough guided horizontal wheels attached to the bus steering. The bus driver would drive the vehicle first on street part of the route as normal, then, on reaching the "guided" section would steer into the trough until the guide wheels contacted the sides of the trough. The driver then released the steering wheel and the bus guided itself along the route. The driver still controlled the speed and braking. Along the experimental section there were six stops (called "Passenger Stations"). At the end of the trough the driver took control of the steering and the vehicle behaved like a standard bus. For the experiment fourteen MCW Metrobus Mark II buses were purchased and fitted with guide wheels. The experiment lasted three years, ending in January 1987, precipitated when the Sunday service was won by a different bus Company that did not agree to the expense of fitting their buses with the necessary steering equipment. As the idea was an experiment it was decided to abandon the guideway and run the buses entirely on the highway. The horizontal guidance wheels were removed from the Tracline 65 buses and the vehicles became ordinary vehicles. The guided bus track was abandoned, the track dismantled and landscaped at a cost of £100,000 (the experiment cost a total of approx. £1M). A driver on the Tracline 65 route commented that the first time he took a bus onto the guided section he had rested his arm through the steering wheel. On reaching the guides the steering wheel kicked around and he thought it was going to break his arm. While there was no publicity about it, given the timing it is possible that Tracline 65 was seen as a potential transport system instead of trams. One notable consequence of the experiment was a rise in passenger numbers on that route of 29% compared to 4% over the rest of the network. This showed Councillors that a fully guided transport, such as a tramway, would be well patronised

THE GUIDED BUS

A NEW APPROACH TO THE PROBLEMS OF URBAN TRANSPORT

Everybody knows that if buses have to move through heavy traffic they add to its congestion and are delayed by it.

You can invest in trains and tubes and even trams. But new tracks are very expensive and only justified when there are enough potential passengers on the route. They also use up urban land which cannot then be used by other traffic. Besides, fixed track systems are not always the best means of catering for passengers with a wide range of destinations.

To find ways of overcoming these problems, and to make bus travel more attractive to car owners, West Midlands Passenger Transport Executive and West Midlands County Council have begun an experiment which is attracting world-wide attention.

The experiment is to enhance one chosen bus route in all possible ways — including a short stretch of special guided bus way. The service operating on this route has been named 'Tracline 65'.

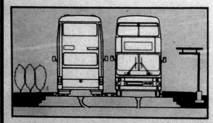

Tracline 65 — the first double-decker guided bus to operate anywhere in the world — is a dual purpose vehicle. On normal roads and routes, it operates freely as a conventional bus. But it can also run on its own special guidance track.

Because the guidance track is reserved exclusively for Tracline 65 buses, there is no other traffic on it — not even other types of bus. So the driver has complete control of his vehicle's speed and punctuality and can concentrate on his passengers' needs. He does not have to steer, except when he enters or leaves the tracked section, or when he has to negotiate major roads that cross the track.

Other traffic is freed from buses having to stop and then pull back into the traffic stream at each bus stop. In fact, because the Guided Bus needs approximately 25% less road space than a normally operated bus, the system can make a contribution to relieving traffic congestion.

And the major long term advantage is that guided tracks can be installed along bus routes wherever they are practicable, as and when finance and circumstances permit.

TRACLINE 65. HOW THE GUIDANCE SYSTEM WORKS

The busway is a twin track with steel guide rails which in this case runs along the central reservation (see the route map). Horizontal guide wheels run along these rails.

The bus enters the track from the ordinary roadway at the beginning of the special section and returns to the ordinary roadway at the end. To enter the system all the driver has to do is steer the bus to bring the offside guide wheel into gentle contact with the leading guide rail. After a short distance the bus engages smoothly with the nearside guide rail and the bus's road wheels are located between the vertical steel guide rails.

THE 65 ROUTE GUIDED SECTION

The 65 Route runs north from Birmingham city centre (Bull Street) to Short Heath via Stockland Green.

The special Tracline 65 experimental guided trackway section extends over 600 metres of double track along Streetly Road's 10 metre wide central reservation which formed part of an old tram route.

Along the 600 metres of trackway, there is one major road intersection. Traffic signals giving bus priority have been installed at the Streetly Road junctions with Short Heath Road, Marlow Road/Edgware Road and Marsh Lane.

Pedestrian crossings are provided at six locations.

There are six bus stops and passenger stations and a new terminus at the outer end of the route at Short Heath.

KEY

- Guided bus way
- Pedestrian crossing point
- Passenger shelters
- Landscaping with new shrubs
- Landscaping with new trees planted
- New total prohibition of waiting
- New limited waiting 11a.m. to 2 p.m. 8am - 6pm Monday to Saturday
- New traffic signals 3 phase
- New traffic signals 2 phase
- Gaps in guideway to provide pedestrian crossing points
- New traffic signals 3 phase
- New pelican crossings
- New traffic signals 3 phase
- Existing traffic signals 3 phase

Not quite a tramway, in March 1984 it was announced that a maglev line was being built to link Birmingham International Railway Station with the terminal buildings of Birmingham Airport. The line opened on 16 August 1984 and provided a free service to the public until July 1995. In 2003 a cable hauled automated people mover called AirRail Link was opened using the same track bed as the Maglev. The AirRail Link

The maglev people mover built to link Birmingham Airport with Birmingham International railway station.

A report "Rapid Transit for the West Midlands", commissioned in 1982, was published on 20 June 1984. This proposed building ten light rail routes combining surface and underground sections (in the city centre) at a cost of £500M. The proposals included changes that were controversial. Four of the suburban railway lines were to be changed to tramway operation with no proposals regarding those existing services reaching beyond the city's boundary. Also the first route from Five Ways to Castle Bromwich, through the city centre with an underground section between Five Ways and a point near the University of Aston, would have required the demolition of 238 houses in the Saltley and Hodge Hill areas. Not surprisingly there was considerable objection from all those with property that could be affected. This was exacerbated by the initial proposals that only identifed a wider area within which the route would take, thus blighting far more than 238 properties. The residents set up a group called "SMART" (Solid Majority Against Rapid Transit) to oppose the scheme. The public opposition to the scheme far outweighed any support that it had. The situation was further confused when the Chairman of the County Transport Committee announced that the Bill to Parliament would only ask for agreement to build the first route. This statement was made without the endorsement of the full Transport Committee. The final straw was the inability of the Council or the Transport Executive to find any Member of Parliament who would sponsor a Bill through Parliament. As a result, the Bill was never lodged, and the scheme was shelved. This was formally decided in April when the Passenger Transport Authority abandoned the proposed Hodge Hill line, thus removing the blight on properties affected, though stating that it was still committed to the concept of light rail.

Following these developments in public transport and the report "Rapid Transit for the West Midlands", serious discussion about rapid transit in the West Midlands began. Then there was another change in the political structure of Local Government. The Local Government Act 1985 saw the West Midlands County Council abolished in March 1986 and the establishment of the West Midlands Passenger Transport Authority, a joint authority of the seven Metropolitan Councils of the West Midlands. It was responsible for setting policies and budgets for public sector transport in the West Midlands County. It has 27 Councillor Members representing the seven Metropolitan Councils. The Joint Authority was advised by the West Mid-lands Passenger Transport Executive (Centro) which implemented the decisions of the PTA. Due to the deregulation legislation, West Midlands Travel was formed in October 1986 from the bus operation of the PTA. It was publicly owned as a subsidiary of the West Midlands PTE, which ceased operating bus services, now having a purely coordinating role. In December 1991 ownership changed when it was sold to management and employees under an Employee Share Ownership Plan. This changed again in April 1995 when it merged with National Express and eighteen months latter was given the brand name "Travel West Midlands".

The Rapid Transit team members that were working for the County Council were transferred to the PTE from 1 April. They were tasked to look at suitable tramway routes in the Black Country with a view to preparing a Parliamentary Bill for late 1987.

It is possible that Coventry Council were feeling rather neglected as in late 1985 the local newspaper published an article saying that plans were being discussed regarding the possibility of using the rail corridors from Nuneaton and Leamington for light rail transit. The suggestions also included a guided busway and a maglev line connecting the city's railway and bus stations.

The idea of a light rail network in the West Midlands continued, but with different proposals to the 1984 scheme. It was envisaged that 15 routes would be built and, optimistically, a date of 1993 was proposed for this network to be operating. Then further routes would be added to complete a 200 kilometres system by the year 2000. The Transport Executive lobbied Members of Parliament, including offering free trips to Grenoble and Hanover to see at first hand those city's tramway networks. Under pressure from local residents the proposals to build a light rail line through Hodge Hill were formally abandoned thus removing the blight that had been created on properties potentially affected by the proposals.

Staff were recruited in the Summer of 1987 to assist in developing proposals for the new scheme. The proposed line was to run from Snow Hill Station to Bilston, with the possibility of running to Wolverhampton using the derelict railway trackbed between Snow Hill and Wolverhampton Low Level. It was expected that the line would open in 1995. The West Midlands PTA held a generous official launch party on 10th September 1987 to announce the introduction of light rail to the West Midlands, conveniently forgetting the fact that there was a similar event in 1984. Possibly learning from the previous attempts, they started by aiming to get politicians and the public on board at an early stage. The formal announcement of the first route of the Metro was made on 16 February 1988, while the Birmingham Council Director of Development stated that in his view rapid transit for the West Midlands was poorly supported and could be an embarrassing failure.

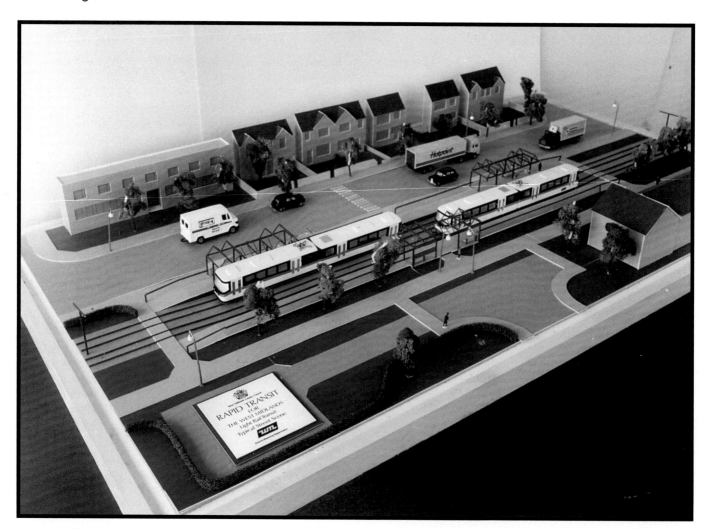

A model made for the County Planning Department of the West Midlands County Council. It was used to demonstrate what a Rapid Transit System could look like in the West Midlands. Photo West Midlands County Council.

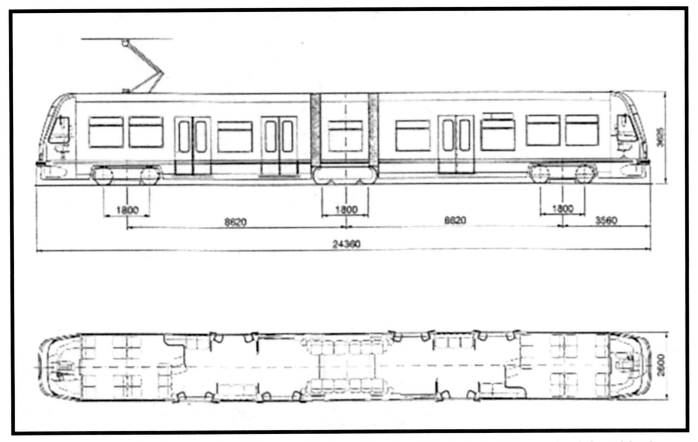

The chosen tram design was the T69 manufactured by Ansaldo in Italy. It transpired that this design was never used on any other tramway, resulting in difficulties in obtaining spares.

At an early stage the proposed Wolverhampton terminus was moved from the Low Level station to a terminus closer to the shopping centre. It was expected that construction would start in 1990. Consultant Engineers were appointed to advise on the network, a possible tunnel under Birmingham City centre and preparing detail for the Low Level route. In November the route in Wolverhampton was announced. The proposal was that the line would leave the reserved track at Stowheath, enter the Bilston Road and run to the inner ring road. A new bridge would be built over the ring road roundabout to carry just the tramway. The line would terminate in Bilston Street.

In order to assist in the development of proposals W. S. Atkins and Mott Hay & Anderson were appointed as Consultant Engineers. Their brief was to advise on the network and particularly possible tunnels and the use of the existing Low Level route track bed. In November 1988 a Bill (Number 1) was deposited in Parliament to build a route from Birmingham Snow Hill Station to Wolverhampton City Centre via West Bromwich, Wednesbury and Bilston. Initially a high floor tramcar was proposed, but this was modified to low floor. Consultants were appointed to advise on financial and corporate issues. Funding was envisaged to be 50% from European Council grants, 25% from central Government and the remainder from the private sector.

The PTE staged an exhibition in Westminster Hall in December. Opened by Peter Snape, MP for West Bromwich East, it displayed plans for a £1,000M, 180km network, built over 20 years, covering Birmingham and the Black Country. The PTE were planning to seek a second Bill to open routes from Five Ways to the NEC and Airport and Wolverhampton to Wednesbury via Walsall. Solihull Council wanted to add an extension from the Airport route to Shirley Station via Solihull town centre. An extension from Walsall to Dudley was added to the proposals. The proposed route in Wolverhampton was detailed. It was to leave the former BR alignment at Stowheath join the public highway on the Bilston Road, to the inner ring road roundabout, cross it on a new bridge and terminate in Bilston Street by the main shopping area.

The first Bill received its Royal Assent on 16 November 1989. The Act included authority to build Line 1 between Snow Hill and Wolverhampton. Having identified the initial route, the West Midlands Passenger Transport Executive commissioned consultants to consider the overall feasibility of the proposals. There was a name change in February 1990 when the WMPTE adopted the name "Centro", which was used in connection with any reference to the Metro. The Number 1 Bill was given its second reading and saw significant support from MPs.

Centro applied to the Department of Transport for a Section 56 grant to help fund part of the estimated £73 million cost. Centro appointed Engineering and Design Consultants to develop the Technical Specifications for Line 1. Centro decided to drop the proposal for a line to go to Stourbridge, instead the application stopped at Dudley. Meanwhile the Bill for lines 2 and 3 was passed through the Opposed Bills Committee with one amendment. The focus of opposition moved to the proposed lines 2 and 3. A leading light of the opposition was "TRAM" (The Residents Against Metro) a local organisation that initially attracted 300 – 400 people to its first meeting, but attendance at later meetings fell to 75. Centro countered by publishing a report showing that noise from the Grenoble tramway was noticeably quieter than buses or lorries going at the same speed.

The Act of Parliament authorising the building of Line 1 of the tramway was given the Royal Assent on 16 November 1989. The line was to run 20 km from Birmingham Snow Hill Station to Wolverhampton city centre going through West Bromwich, Wednesbury and Bilston. A second Bill was submitted to Parliament for lines 2 and 3 at the end of the month. A new bus station was proposed at Bilston that would be an interchange with Line 1. Now Centro needed to get the financial support needed to build the tramway.

In April 1990 Centro applied to Government for a £1.5 million grant for the preliminary development and granting of the contract for construction and initial operation. This was agreed and then Central Government added a further £3 million in March 1992. At the same time Royal Assent was given for Line 2 from Birmingham city centre to the airport. Centro announced that an application would be made for Line 3 from Wolverhampton to Walsall.

Notices started appearing along the route of the tramway early in 1998 announcing that the Metro would open in the Summer. These were somewhat premature, as was the yellow livery used on the posters.

Centro set about seeking funding for the project. Precise figures for the scheme are not available, however the financial sums were stated at 1995 prices and do not reflect some of the reductions in specifications or additional projects built after the opening. The bulk of the money, £80M, was to come from central Government, with a large sum, £31M from the European Regional Development Fund; £17M from The West Midlands Passenger Transport Authority, £10M from the Altram consortia, £4M from Birmingham, Sandwell and Wolverhampton Councils Development Corporations, £2M savings agreed with Altram and £1M from sales of Centro land and property; a total of £145M. The major change for the public was the reduction of the length of the tramcars. Cost savings measures had to be implemented including the decision to reduce expenditure by not having the centre sections for the T69 tramcars.

The winning consortia consisted of Ansaldo Transporti (tramcar constructor) and Taylor Woodrow, civil engineers. Later John Laing Construction replaced Taylor Woodrow. The Anglo-Italian consortia was granted a 23 year contract consisting of three years construction and 20 years of operation and maintenance. The contract was agreed in August 1995 and construction began three months later. In 1996 Travel West Midlands joined the consortium.

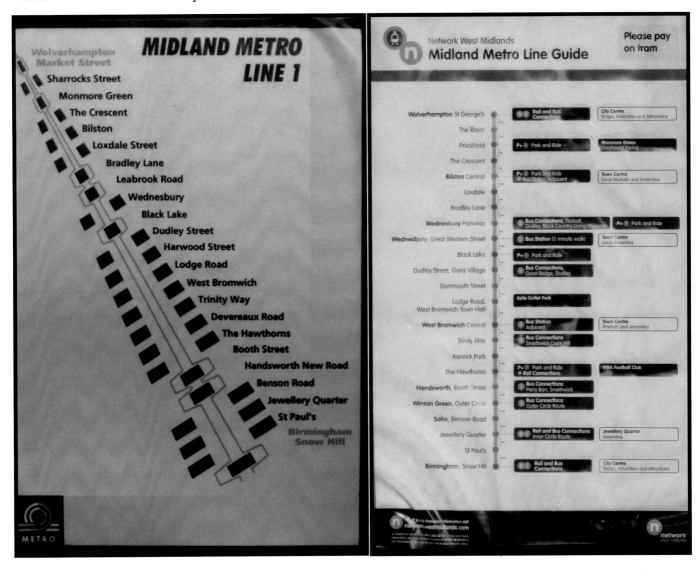

Posters advertising the line that were displayed during construction and soon after completion. Note the change of name for the following stops:- "Wolverhampton Market Street" became "Wolverhampton St Georges"; "Sharrock Street" became "The Royal"; "Monmore Green" became "Priestfield"; "Bilston" became "Bilston Central"; "Loxdale Street" became "Loxdale"; "Leabrook Road" became "Wednesbury Parkway"; "Wednesbury Great Western Street" is a new stop; "Dudley Street" became "Dudley Street Gunns Village"; "Harwood Street"became "Dartmouth Street"; "Lodge Road" gained the words "West Bromwich Town Hall"; "West Bromwich" became "West Bromwich Central"; "Devereaux Road" became "Kenrick Park" ; "Booth Street" became "Handsworth Booth Street"; "Handsworth New Road" became "Winson Green Outer Circle" and "Benson Road" became "Soho Benson Road". The note asking customers to pay on the tram reflects the problems encountered with ticket machines after the line had opened for passengers.

The inside of the mock-up tram showing the two level floor needed to give sufficient room for the power bogies. The electric fire was not part of the standard fittings!

CHAPTER 2

Construction of the new Tramway Route 1995 - 1998

At this point it is helpful to examine the complexities of the interactions between the organisations involved in the ownership, building and operation of the Midland Metro. Under the Transport Act 1968, implemented on 1 October 1969, the responsibility for the operation and coordination of public transport in large conurbations was vested in Public Transport Executives (PTE's). In the West Midlands, the West Midlands PTE was given the responsibility for public passenger transport in its area. The area including the City of Birmingham, the County Boroughs of Dudley, Solihull, Walsall, Warley, West Bromwich and Wolverhampton (later to become a city), plus those parts of Staffordshire, Warwickshire and Worcestershire adjacent to the PTE area. It included all the public bus operations, and railway services in the area. The PTE also had responsibility for any tramway services built in its area.

Around this time, the thoughts of many cities were turning to the idea of modern tramways to help solve the ever increasing problems created by road congestion. However, remembering the adverse public reaction to the old tramways (particularly when systems were badly run down because of the war) there was reluctance to use the term tramway. So, when looking at proposals for new tramways, the names used were "Rapid Transit", "Light Railway", "Metro" or even "Supertram". Proposals for new systems all incorporated routes with their own right of way. In the cases of Tyne and Wear Metro and the Docklands Light Railway the routes are entirely on their own right of way and have no road running.

The Grant Rail tracklaying train on the northbound track at Winson Green Outer Circle tram stop on 8 July 1997. It is in the charge of RMS Locotec Hire loco H015 - a Hunslet 0-6-0D (7410 of 1977). The contractors have built the foundation for the island platform at this stop and the rails for the southbound line are in their concrete base but are temporarily covered with a layer of sand to enable road tyred vehicles to pass over them to gain access to the trackbed. The buffer stop at the left is at the end of the headshunt for Queens Head Sidings. The skew bridge in the background carries the Network Rail Perry Barr to Soho line over the Metro line and the parallel Jewellery Line. Photo Roger Monk.

As has been previously detailed, the delays to the West Midlands proposals following the initial application for the Government Grant to provide essential funding for the project were extremely frustrating. The first application for funding was made in 1990. It was rejected by the Government that year and in the following two years. It appeared that the Government had a policy of funding no more than one light rail scheme a year and the Midlands Metro was in a queue behind the Manchester Metrolink and Sheffield Supertram.

Contractors laying the pointwork near the former Metro terminus in Snow Hill Station on 18 August 1997. The short single track section from near the St Pauls stop into the station occupied a former single line heavy rail terminal platform (the edge of which is seen at the left of the photo), capped with a new brick edg-ing. There was insufficient space here to continue the double track light rail formation but it was possible to provide two termi-nal stubs for the Metro either side of a new island platform adja-

Despite the lack of the government's firm commitment to provide funding for the line, in 1993 tenders were invited from Companies to build the line. Four tenders were selected for consideration. These were Balfour Beatty and Siemens; Centram; John Mowlem and GEC; Alsthom; and Eurotransi. They were all invited to go forward to the next stage. On 17 May it was announced that Centram, a consortia of Ansaldo and Taylor Woodrow, were appointed to design, build, operate and maintain line 1, Ansaldo being an Italian tramcar manufacturer. The contract was to last 23 years, consisting of a 3 year build and 20 years operation. The tramway was to operate as private Company with no subsidy. Some advance work had already been carried out between Snow Hill and The Hawthorns at a cost of £3 million. The contract specified that the service frequency was to be every 6 minutes.

However, on 28 June 1993 the Taylor Woodrow Board failed to endorse the contract agreed and signed by its negotiators on 20 June. Centro immediately began negotiations with other bidders, but Ansaldo said they were ready to take on the whole of the route 1 project themselves, meeting all conditions set out in contract. In February 1994, John Laing joined Ansaldo as joint contractors to build and operate the Midland Metro, a £102 mil-lion project. The new consortia was named Altram (A for Ansaldo and L for Laing).

The Passenger Transport Executive expected government funding to be approved in November 1994. On this basis construction could start immediately with an operational date of 1998. It was not until 13 December 1994 that Dr Brian Mawhinney, the then Secretary of State for Transport, gave government approval, subject to the agreement of the Local Authorities to the route and a contribution towards the funding. He allocated £5 million to enable a start to be made in 1995/6 with the system due to open in 1998. He said that more funds would have to be found from local sources such as the Birmingham City Council selling its shares in Birmingham airport. When a delegation of local Councils met with the Secretary of State in January 1995 he stated that funding for the scheme would be £100 million including local borrowing. It was up to the Councils, Centro and Altram to fund the gap. By August 1995 Centro had found new cash to meet the shortfall of £21.4 million between the promised funding and the forecast cost (£124 million and £145 mil-lion). However, the Government insisted on some cost savings through reductions in the scope of the scheme, particularly by removing three of the stops and reducing the size of the tramcars.

Seen on 7 July 1997, this is one of the temporary yards where the track panels were assembled from rails and sleepers brought to the site by road. The Donelli gantries (one of a pair seen here) running on 'broad gauge' rails were used to assemble and then load the track panels onto the track-laying train. This one was at the Winson Green Outer Circle Stop. Note how the rails at the stops were laid first and fixed into the concrete foundations. These sections received rails rolled to a harder specification than the rest of the running rails in order to resist wear from the cars braking and accelerating. The buffer stop on the left marks the end of the headshunt for Network Rail's Queens Head Sidings. Photo Roger Monk.

The Metro flyover at Queens Head Sidings between the Winson Green and Booth Street stops. This flyover was necessitated by the requirement to avoid a level crossing of the Metro line and the access from the Network Rail main line (seen on the left in this view, behind the blue fencing) into these sidings. The latter were used to facilitate shunting and run round movements into and out of a cramped siding on the other side of the main line that served a scrap yard. In recent times the latter has closed but the sidings on this side of the line are still maintained in usable condition. Photo Roger Monk.

The track between stops came ready assembled from temporary yards along the route and was laid in a similar way to model railway track. Here, at Soho, Benson Road, a length of track is lifted from its wagon by a specialised machine. The four wheel wagon in the foreground was used to transport the tracklaying machine to the worksite. Numbered Grant Rail 5084 it is thought to be one of only five 'train ferry-fitted' 27.5t conflats that were built in 1984 for STS. It is believed the ferry traffic for them was non-existent; apart from a brief period in 1987 they saw little use on the main line. Photo Roger Monk.

Having been moved into place the section of track was lowered and bolted to rails already laid on the southbound track. The remote controlled (by the operator on the right) trackbed machine was named Amica (a girls name of Latin origin). In the background a tamping machine is working on the already laid northbound track. Photo Roger Monk.

There was a formal signing of documents on 3 August 1995 at the Hawthorns Railway Station, which enabled work to begin on building the Metro. The Government funded the project to the level of £145 million. A spokesman for the Government said "It has taken eight years to get this far and takes national investment in Light Rail since the mid-1970s over the £1000 million mark." The contracts with Altram were signed. The project had funding of £145 million, comprising £80 million Government grant, £31 million European Regional Development Fund grant, £17 million from the West Midlands PTA, £10 million Altram, £4 million Birmingham, Sandwell and Wolverhampton Councils Development Corporation, £2 million savings agreed with Altram, and £1 million from sales of Centro land and property.

The building work was officially started on Monday 13 November 1995 and was expected to be completed by August 1998, some ten years after Parliamentary Approval had been granted. The location chosen for the turf cutting ceremony was the site of the West Bromwich Town stop. It was selected for the ease of access for the media, as the actual construction work had started at the Wednesbury depot, several miles away. It was tempting fate to choose the 13th for the ceremony and, as will be described, the tramway seems to have been dogged by bad luck ever since. The ceremony included a formal cutting of the first sod, in this instance using a JCB. The guests for the ceremony were Transport Secretary, Sir George Young, and Councillor Worrall (Chair, West Midlands Passenger Transport Authority), neither of whom were conversant with the controls of a JCB. The usual driver had to give instruction. However, the cab of the digger was designed for one person and unable to accommodate all three. Just prior to the ceremony, Sir George Young was photographed leaving the vehicle gesturing towards the two that remained in the cab. It seems that this was not an auspicious start to the development. In reality, preparatory work had already started some weeks before between The Hawthorns and Snow Hill. It was announced that the line would open in the summer of 1998.

The machines used in the construction came from a variety of sources. Here the rail lorry on the left is a Robel Rail one owned by the contractor Grant Rail, while the on track plant on the right is a road/rail Atlas 1604K machine hired for this contract. These are seen at work at Handsworth Booth Street on 30 September 1997. Photo Roger Monk.

The main contractor for the building of the trackwork and stops was John Laing, a large company well used to this sort of project. At the time of building the Midland Metro, Laing was also undertaking contracts for Ashford International Station for Eurostar and the Eurohub Terminal at Birmingham Airport. One of the less welcome surprises found in the Black Country area was the discovery of old and unrecorded mine shafts. The Metro was not immune and several old shafts were found along the route, all of which had to be capped. Indeed, during track renewal at "The Royal" stop in 2014 an old mine shaft was discovered that was believed to date back to the industrial revolution. Work was delayed by several weeks while remedial work was undertaken. The route was to be double track throughout, except for the approach to Snow Hill Station where there was insufficient room due to support pillars for the multi-storey car park and the approach to the tramway platform was single track ending in a double track stub. Pedestrians entered or left the platform by stairs, lift or escalator to reach the ground level floors or by a pedestrian crossing leading to the station's other platforms.

The track bed of the tramway intruded into the long closed to new burials Key Hill Cemetery in the Jewellery Quarter. This required the reinternment of some graves in another part of the cemetery. The overhead wiring train is seen with Grant Rail Ruston Hornsby 0-4-0D number 6 on 3 April 1998

The Route Described

Travelling north, the line leaves Snow Hill station on a single line that became double just before St Pauls stop. A new stop was built at the Jewellery Quarter where the line ran alongside a disused cemetery. A portion of land was required from the cemetery. This entailed relocating remains from graves that were disturbed and reburying them elsewhere in the cemetery. The next issue for the tramway was at Cooper's Scrapyard, Handsworth, where sidings from the railway crossed the intended path of the tramway. These sidings were used weekly to take scrap to either Aldwarke or Cardiff. Cooper's siding was on the south side of the Jewellery Line but was fairly cramped so, in order to do the shunt to change over between the empty and full wagons and for the loco to run round its train, use had to be made of the sidings (known as Queens Head Sidings) serving the former cement terminal on the north side of the line here. This arrangement facilitated minimal disruption to the frequent passenger trains using the Jewellery Line. British Rail insisted that the tramway could not cross it on the level. Instead, a long flyover had to be built at a cost of £2.7 million, the most expensive structure on the whole tramway.

Bilston Central stop was located a little north of the original Bilston Station, bringing it close to the bus station. Set in a very limited cutting the platforms had to be staggered and a lift installed to allow access. However, there was not enough room for two lifts, only one was provided built on the bus station side. Though there are stairs it can be difficult when the lift is out of order for those less able passengers to get to and from the platforms.

The tramway route joins the Bilston Road soon after the Priestfield stop. From here the tramway runs along the public highway to reach The Royal and the terminus at Wolverhampton, St Georges. Inevitably the construction work disrupted the busy traffic with one-way sections controlled by traffic lights. On the route, a little before the terminus, was a large roundabout that was part of the inner ring road. Rather than have trams making their way around the road, the decision was taken to allow the tram to cross the sunk-en centre of the roundabout on a bridge. This was given a most distinctive "wishbone" design. In order to protect the trams and other road vehicles from each other, the access to the bridge was protected by traffic lights that stopped the road traffic to allow the tram a safe passage across to the bridge.

One of the short lived ticket machines being carried to position at one of the stops. The failure of the machines lost the tramway significant revenue and were replaced with Customer Service Representatives who travel on the trams and sell tickets to passengers. Photo Roger Monk.

Work is nearing completion at Bilston Central. Located in a cutting the limited space meant that the platforms had to be staggered and there was room for only one passenger lift, which has proved a difficulty when it is being maintained or has broken down. The stairs are distinctly disabled unfriendly. Photographed 1999.

It is interesting to compare the construction of today's generation of tramways and that when tramways were a very new idea. When tramways were first being laid around the 1900s the technology of the time was to use man power with just picks, shovels and wheel barrows. Today there are lots of machines and far fewer men. Building the Metro was no exception, machinery was used extensively. Many of the Companies involved in the building of the tramway had their own range of specialist vehicles, or would hire suitable vehicles. A range of road, rail and road-rail vehicles were used, all designed to speed the con-struction of the tramway. One interesting aspect of this is the way the vehicles got to the tramway. It may be thought that the railed vehicles would be transported over the railway network to the metro. However, this is not the case. The road and road-rail vehicles can be driven to the construction site. But the dedicated rail-only equipment has to be taken in another way. Well not really, they do travel by road, but on the back of specialist carrying vehicles. This chapter includes photos of some of the unusual vehicles used in the construction of the Metro.

Once work on the alignment of the route was completed, it was possible to start laying the track. This was started at the depot at Wednesbury and work went in both the Birmingham and Wolverhampton directions. The contract for track laying had was given to Grant Rail. The first track to be laid was at the stops. It is believed that this was due to a harder wearing rail being used, because that rail was embedded in block paving, all laid on a concrete base and not on sleepers like the track between stops. The rails running next to the platforms at the stops were laid so that there was a 40mm gap between the tram and the platform. This was small enough not to cause any issues for the passengers while allowing the tram to tilt due to passengers waiting at the doorway. All the stops were built to be level and straight (except Bilston Central that is laid on a curve). Where possible the area around each stop was landscaped with gardens to be as attractive as possible. A total of 82,000 trees and 113,000 shrubs were planted. Each stop has closed circuit television so that the central control room can see any behaviour that needs controlling. If required the control operator can switch on a loudspeaker and inform miscreants that they have been observed and that the police are on their way.

The £2.7M viaduct constructed to avoid the railway siding to a scrap yard, which closed around 2016. A Central Trains class 150 dmu passes on the Jewellery Line as the Grant Rail track laying train, working from Wednesbury, is on the flyover propelled by ex ICI D3 hire loco, a Thomas Hill built (167v of 1966) 0-6-0DH on 20 June 1997. This was the first movement by a train over the flyover. Photo Roger Monk.

One difficulty that appeared early on was caused by rainwater. Because the stops are level rain tends to accumulate and on some occasions this caused stray currents that interfered with electrical and telephone cables. The solution was to remove the track and block paving and lay a sheet of heavy duty insulation then relay everything. This prevented the stray currents. Difficulty was also encountered on the overhead wiring. Along most of the route the overhead wiring was installed with a double contact wire.

On 19 January 1996 West Midlands Travel (part of the National Express Group) was announced as the chosen operator for the Tramway. Towards the end of 1996 a mock-up of one section of the proposed tramcars was delivered and displayed at the Wednesbury depot stop during November. Then during December it went on a tour to West Bromwich, Birmingham and Wolverhampton. It was slightly unusual in having a different livery on each side of the vehicle. The main colour was yellow but each side of the car were different shades of yellow. The members of the general public were invited to vote for which of the shades they preferred. Typically for such consultation of the population by public bodies, the livery finally chosen was red, yellow and blue, designed by Ray Stenning (designer of many modern liveries seen on public transport in the UK). The decision to change the livery was made by the PTA's Midland Metro Work-ing Party. A vote was taken which was equally split between the yellow livery voted by the public and the one by the professional designer. The Chairman of the Group used his casting vote to support the purple livery. It is not known exactly when the decision was taken, but tram number 3 had been given the yellow livery when constructed in September 1997. It was repainted in the "Purple People Mover" col-ours before leaving Italy. The first tramcar in the new livery was displayed in the manufacturer's yard in January 1998.

The original Metro route 1 started at the terminus at a stop in Bilston Street named Wolverhampton St Georges. It then ran across the Wolverhampton Ring Road roundabout to the Bilston Road, which was a route on the old Wolverhampton Corporation tramway. The Metro leaves the road at Priestfield to go on its own private right of way, previously the track bed of the Great Western main line to Wolverhampton Low Level Station. Going south the route runs parallel to the A41, Wellington Road, to its junction with the A4098, Great Bridge Road, which it runs parallel with until crossing it to run on open land past Wednesbury to parallel the A4196, Holloway Bank, to Dudley Street, Guns Village. Here it goes through an urban area to reach The Hawthorns station, where the Kidderminster railway line joins it to run parallel into Snow Hill Railway Station. The last part of the tramway ran single track into Snow Hill station due to limited space. At the terminus there was a double track with the platform between the tracks. There were two significant bridges that were part of the route. The most attractive by far was the "wishbone" bridge taking the Metro line over the roundabout on the Wolverhampton Ring Road. Strictly for the Metro only, trams crossing the bridge are protected by traffic signals. The central area of the rounda-bout is lower, providing access for pedestrians to cross the road junctions. The other structure is a viaduct between Handsworth Booth Street and Winson Green Outer Circle stops. This was insisted upon by British Rail to cross a siding from the Snow Hill line that was used to serve Cooper's scrap merchant. To ensure a gentle gradient for the trams the structure is some length. Without knowing the full story, it appears that the railway insisted on complete separation between their railway line (calling it a "strategic rail siding") and any tramway rails, despite the siding only having been used about once a week. The cost was £2.7M, the most expensive structure for the tramway. Ironically, the scrap yard closed a few years later and the siding is currently unused, though still maintained. Construction of the track and stops were completed by early 1998 and the route was ready for service.

The Hawthorns tram stop under construction. It is alongside the railway station, but fenced off to prevent passengers wandering between the two. It was used for one of the pre-opening exercises when two fully loaded trams arrived at the same time to replicate the conditions on a match day at the West Bromwich Albion ground.

In 1996, for the population of Birmingham and Wolverhampton, the first sign that they were about to get a tramway was the appearance on 22 November of a mock-up of half a tramcar. Here in front of Birmingham Town Hall it attracts the attention of passing pedestrians. It was also displayed by the depot at Wednesbury. In November 1996 It then went on a tour of West Bromwich, Birmingham and Wolverhampton during December. Photo Roger Monk.

CHAPTER 3

Troublesome Trams 1998—1999

The contract required the tramway to be operational by 2nd August 1998. The trackwork and structural elements were on schedule. However, there were significant difficulties with the tramcars. Designed as partially low floor vehicles, with low floor access for 60% of the vehicle (they were built before the now required 100% low floor designs). Designated Class T69 the sixteen tramcars were unique as they were the only tramcars ever built to this design. This was later to create problems with the availability of spares. The Tramway was to discover that each tramcar was built with its own particular (and peculiar) modifications. Externally they looked the same, but inside there were many differences especially in the mechanical and electrical work. This led to the maintenance staff having to undertake extensive modifications, repairs and replacement work to suit each tramcar before they could enter service. It was reported that the main power cables from the pantograph were laid through underfloor compartments and inspections discovered that the cable was not only unprotected but also had an uninsulated joint hanging close to the metal floor of the compartment it passed through. With just sixteen vehicles in the whole world, Ansaldo did not keep a stock of spare parts. When a component failed or was damaged and needed replacement an order would be placed. Usually it would need to be manufactured, which took time, during which the tramcar could be out of service. Indeed, at one stage a tramcar that had a major component failure would be parked at the back of the depot and used as a source of spares to keep others in service. Such a tram was referred to as a "Christmas Tree" as it gave presents to other trams. The first "Christmas Tree" was tram 07 which was waiting for spares following a major accident in 2000. Later Tram number 01 broke down and the necessary parts were unobtainable for some time. So it also acted as the source of spares. The next tram to become unserviceable due to technical problems was tram 02 and both vehicles became "Christmas Trees",

The depot at Wednesbury with a tram just visible in the building on 2 June 1998. Vehicles used for the construction and maintenance of the tramway are parked outside: a Unimog/Mercedes Road/Rail on its miniature rail wheels and a six wheel Iveco road/rail vehicle, which is still unregistered, following delivery on a low loader on 19 May. It later received registration number R199 EOX. It was supplied with a snow plough attachment. Photo Roger Monk.

The delivery of the trams was protracted with the first tramcar, number 01, not reaching Wednesbury until 14 February 1998. Unloaded from the low loader the tramway management eagerly opened the doors and stepped inside. Inside only to find the interior entirely bare and it was without power. With no seats and no means of moving itself, the tramcar had to be pushed out of the depot building on 19 February 1998 to be inspected by the waiting Press. It was clear that the tramcar needed a significant amount of work before it was ready to enter service. Tram number 02 arrived at Wednesbury on 12th May. Unlike tram 01, the interior of this one had passenger seats, handrails and cab interior doors. Rumours that tram 01 was an experimental "standing only" tram were unfounded! Seats for tram number 01 were sent from Italy a little later. It was becoming apparent that the hoped-for opening of the Tramway was very likely going to be delayed.

Just south of St Pauls stop the tramway went to single track in order to enter Snow Hill station. The tramcar has yet to be given a number and has a blank destination indicator. Note the railway distance marker to the right of the tram that shows the distance to London Paddington is 129 miles. Photo Roger Monk.

With the start of tramcars arriving thoughts turned to recruiting staff. Advertisements were placed for tram drivers. It had already been decided that there would be no conductors as each stop had a ticket machine on each of the platforms. Tickets would be pre-purchased and inspectors would check for fare evasion. An early decision had been taken that every member of staff would be trained to drive the trams and would be expected to regularly take on driving duties. Recruitment took place in early 1998 and training started in April. However, no trams were available and so the first trainees were given driver training on the Sheffield South Yorkshire Supertram system.

The first tram to run in Wolverhampton for about 70 years reached St Georges terminus on Thursday, 3 September 1998 (the stop was named after nearby St Georges church that became redundant in 1978 and was converted into a Sainsbury's store in 1986, now relocated to near the Ring Road, St Marks). The vehicle was number 06 and it arrived about 11.00hrs. On Friday 4 September further runs took place with car 03. Whilst waiting at Wolverhampton the tramcar attracted favourable comment from passing pedestrians. This was followed by a number of test runs held over two days for the benefit of the Inspectorate of Railways section of the Health & Safety Executive. On each run the tram was followed by two patrol cars from the British Transport Police. Stephen Firth, Inspector of Railways for the region, gave a favourable response to the tests and commented "I am happy with the way the tests went. The main purpose of this run was to check that the train (*sic*) fitted the infrastructure properly and it did." The appearance of the tram prompted Rev Tony Kinch, Minister of Darlington Street Methodist Church, to give the tram an impromptu blessing. More runs, at scheduled speed, then took place to test signalling and other equipment.

Early in 1998 it was becoming apparent that the hoped-for opening of the Tramway was very likely going to be deferred. One of the tramcars had suffered a leak allowing water to seep into the tram body and that had soaked part of the electrical system. The Rail Inspectorate halted the trial running until the fault was identified and rectified and every tramcar was inspected to determine if any other car had a similar fault. During one of the inspections by the Rail Inspectorate it was discovered that the windscreen wipers on the tramcars did not clear a sufficient area of the windscreen. This was rectified by removing the single wiper blade and replacing it with two blades joined by a short bar, the result looking like a capital letter "H". In addition there was another, more serious matter, because a number of issues arose that meant that the delivery of the tramcars was becoming more protracted, much to the dismay of the tramway management. The lack of an interior in car number 01 meant much finishing work had to be carried out and it was not ready for testing until September 1998. The last tram, number 16, did not arrive until March 1999.

Tram 02 with the modified "H" windscreen wipers necessary to meet the new regulations. Later these were replaced by longer single blades. The tram is at West Bromwich Central stop. The locomotive driving wheels commemorate that this was the site of the West Bromwich (GWR) Station.

Adjacent to the St Pauls stop the Grant Rail Ballasting train is hauled by RMS Locotec hire loco HO 15 on 8 September 1997. The train consists of two veteran former Southern Railway Walrus bogie ballast wagons and three former revenue service (for aggregate etc. traffic) BR TOPS coded PGA wagons hopper wagons. On the other Metro track is a ballast tamping machine. Photo Roger Monk.

The physical delivery of the trams was also experiencing problems. Overland transport was disrupted by travel bans, bad weather and unavailability of police escorts meaning that trams 03, that arrived on 17 June 1998, and 04, arriving 30 June, were delivered, still on their trailers, by sea from the port of Caserta to Bristol. From Bristol the tram still on its trailer was hauled by a British articulated lorry to Wednesbury. A more cheerful note was experienced when 02 was approved by HMRI for driver training on 16 June on the Wednesbury to West Bromwich section. West Midland PTA (Centro) expressed disappointment at the delay in opening the line and said it intended to claim damages for the delay. It seemed that only nine trams would be available for service by the end of October which were only enough for a ten-minute service, the full service needing fifteen trams.

On 7 July car 01 was given a test run, albeit being pushed by a road/rail lorry. Only one tram was available for training duties and the programme began to overrun. Car 05 missed its boat and had to be taken overland, arriving early July with car 06 arriving on July 27 having made the sea voyage. The HMRI insisted on a considerable number of modifications to meet UK requirements. A programme of rectification was immediately put in place.

An agreement was signed with British Transport Police for them to provide a policing service on the tramway. The immediate effect of police presence was to reduce the number of incidents of vandalism. Trams 07, 08, 09, and 10 arrived in August and September 1998. On 3 September the test runs in Wolverhampton streets began with a representative from HM Inspectorate riding on the car. In October the Railway Inspectorate cleared the whole line for test running. A staged programme of driver familiarisation was approved by the Railway Inspectorate, with training and later a full timetable trial operation. Beginning on 26 October authorisation was given for street running without a police escort. Trams 11, 12, and 13 arrived on 6 October, 16 October and 23 October respectively. In order to speed up driver training two instructors were hired from Sheffield Stagecoach Supertram. Altram announced a new date for the opening of the tramway, 18 January 1999. However, news from Ansaldo indicates that there would be further delays in deliveries. The manufacturer did agree to modify the remaining trams to meet HMRI requirements.

A specialised road-rail motor with a trailer carrying drums of lineside wiring is seen near Wednesbury Parkway stop on 19 February 1998 during the final stages of construction. The pointwork leads to the depot. Photo Roger Monk.

Grant Rail loco number 6 (Ruston and Hornsby 165DE type 421435 of 1958) parked adjacent to Wednesbury Depot on 19 February 1998 in charge of GR5082, an ex London Underground Railway flat wagon fitted with a framework probably for gauging tests along the route. Photo Roger Monk.

The Company wanted to ensure that the system would be able to cope with various incidents. In November 1998 the public was asked for volunteers to join a series of exercises to simulate various emergency situations. Towards the end of the year and the beginning of 1999, several incidents were arranged, with trams full of volunteers. These included a simulated derailed tramcar (number 05) in the Hill Top Tunnel where the passengers were transferred to a relief tramcar (number 07). Later a simulated fire under tramcar number 04 brought it to a halt between Dartmouth Street and Lodge Road. The fire brigade was called and attended. The Brigade officers were shown how to make the live overhead safe prior to using hoses. The driver contacted the control room, and the power was cut off. To ensure it was kept earthed and safe the driver pulled a long pole from under the car that was fitted with a thick wire. He clipped one end of the wire to a rail and lifted the other end and hooked it over the overhead wire, thus ensuring it was safe if power had been reconnected while the firefighters sprayed water over the tram. The third exercise was somewhat larger. The tramway wanted to see the consequences of two trams arriving at the Hawthorns at the same time bringing football fans to a West Bromwich Albion match. It was arranged that a full tram from the north (car 06) arrived at the same time as a full tram (car 09) from the south. All the "passengers" had been given replica tickets for the exercise, though the task of checking tickets proved difficult. Following the exodus from the station the passengers returned to the platform and were asked to get as many people into a single tram as possible. The crush loading of the tramcars was given as 102 standing and 56 seated. As one of the volunteers I can report that it felt like a lot more! The final exercise took place on Sunday 28 February when tram number 13 came to a halt near the Jewellery Quarter stop. The simulation was of a gas leak requiring the tramcar to be evacuated and the passengers to be moved to a safer place.

There were other exercises carried out for the staff but without public participation. During a late evening the tramway carried out an exercise near the end of the private right of way approaching the Bilston Road. It was carried out in the presence of Altram and Health and Safety Officials. As the exercise was carried out on the private right of way the Tramway had not told the police that it was taking place. This resulted in a complaint from them for not being informed.

Members of staff and management gained valuable experience from the exercises and were able to modify their emergency procedures in the light of the experiences. The whole thing was fun for all the volunteers, who all had the pleasure of riding the trams before the official opening date. Though they were not the only ones. It was not unknown for tramcars on driver training to stop at a platform and for a member of the public to board and get a free ride along the route.

Making the overhead safe during the simulated fire exercise . The volunteer passengers were es-corted away from the tram for safety. The cold and wet weather were not always appreciated.

Simulation of a football crowd arriving at The Hawthorns for a match at the West Bromwich football ground. We were waiting for a second tram coming in the opposite direction to test the crowd control procedures.

A testing run on 19 August 1998 soon after delivery. The tram (possibly car 3) that has yet to be numbered, is at Swan Lane level crossing (near Black Lake). The lower front panel of the car has yet to be fitted. Note the hand-worked temporary barriers and temporary traffic lights to control the crossing. Photo Roger Monk.

Altram had a policy that all staff pass as drivers so that they can be called on at any time to keep the service running. Part of the scheme meant that management and administrative staff could drive trams and needed to have regular experience to keep their driving skills up to date. However, poor tram availability had an adverse effect on driver training.

48 ticket machines were purchased from Italy and two will be allocated to each stop, one on each platform except Snow Hill and Wolverhampton St Georges where extra machines would be fitted. The intention was that the only employee on the trams would be the driver. Roving inspectors would randomly ride on trams in order to check tickets and issue fines to those riding without paying. These ticket machines were to be another major cause for concern.

In 1990, Midland Metro Line One's build cost was put at around £60 million, but that figure turned out to be a severe underestimate. The project had to be de-scoped, with the number of stops cut from 27 to 23, and two-section trams ordered instead of three-section ones. Despite specification downgrades, the official statement about the price was that it was £145 million "at 1995 prices". The exact cost has never been revealed as it was "commercially sensitive", often a euphemism for "embarrassing". The funding that was made public was found from interested parties. Central Government grants and loans accounted for £80m, with an additional £31m coming from the European Regional Development Fund. The West Midlands Passenger Transport Authority, the region's statutory local transport provider, provided £17.1m, while Altram contributed £11.4m. This accounts for £139.5m, but the year that these figures relate to has not been made clear.

The contract to build Metro included a provision that 1% of budget had to be set aside for Arts projects. The most prominent element of this requirement was the installation of a large stainless steel effigy of a mythical horse. It was erected on a hill overlooking the Wednesbury depot (it cost £11,000). It portrays Sleipir, the eight legged steed of Odin, the Norse God. Other projects included a special song for the Metro opening (costing £40,000 and raised much criticism) and a special lighting scheme on the Wishbone bridge at Wolverhampton. A spokesman commented that it was a pity that those Councillors who were critical had not objected when the proposals were discussed before the money was committed.

Car 04 on the single track approach to Snow Hill Station on a crisp winter's afternoon.

The control room at the depot where any incidents are managed.

Overlooking the depot is a statue of the mythical eight legged horse of Norse legend "Sleipir".

The delays in the delivery of the tramcars were frustrating for the tramway management. An additional concern was that the contract for building the tramway had penalty clauses. Any failure to meet the planned opening date incurred a financial penalty of £24,000 for each day beyond the programmed start date. By early April 1999 this had reached £3.6M. It is not clear what was the final sum reached for the nine month delay, nor what proportion was actually paid. The information has been hidden behind the excuse of "commercial confidentiality".

The delay in the tramway opening also had an unfortunate consequence. On 1 January 1999 the Rail Vehicle Accessibility Regulations came into force. As the Midland Metro had not commenced public operation, it now became subject to the new regulations. This meant that the tramcars did not comply with the new regulations. The letters on the passenger displays in the tramcars indicating the next stop had to comply with the new regulations, but those installed in the trams were 3mm too small. The regulators allowed the tramway time to install new indicators to meet the regulations. A programme of replacement was agreed where the new indicators were installed by April 2001. The regulations also changed regarding wheelchair access. Wheelchairs had to be provided with room to park facing the direction of travel (the provision in the tramcars allowed parking at right angles to travel).

There was a public meeting between the Passenger Transport Authority and Altram, where representatives of Altram refused to answer questions regarding the problems that had arisen. They said they would only do so behind closed doors.

The Her Majesty's Railway Inspectorate (HMRI) had required that new handrails and wheelchair constraints should be fitted in order to meet health and safety rules. The modifications were checked by the HMRI and approved. Altram launched a campaign, titled "Experience Waitless Travel" emphasising the frequency of the tram service. On 5 May, to celebrate the end of the construction phase, the lights on the Wishbone bridge were switched on.

As the tramway was built on the old railway line, much of which was in cuttings, it was not readily visible to pedestrians. Close to the opening date it was realised that signposts were needed to guide the pubic to the tram stops. It was initially proposed that the tramway could open in two phases, starting with the section from Wednesbury to Birmingham. However, it was decided that the whole line should open as one unit. On 13 May 1999 the HMRI approved the opening of the line and it was announced that the tramway would open to the public on the Spring Bank Holiday weekend 30 May 1999. But the system's bad luck continued, with tram number 03 being struck by lightning three days before the opening while travelling near Bradley Lane during a storm. The strike burnt a hole in the roof and destroyed much of the cabling putting the tram out of service for many weeks. The lightening arrester appears to have been disabled and the force of the electricity had severely damaged much electrical equipment.

The formal opening took place on the Sunday 30 May 1999 with an official tram (07) leaving Snow Hill after breaking a banner. It broke further banners at stops on the way to Wolverhampton. There was also a blessing by Railway Mission Chaplain, Rev. John Bassett, at the West Bromwich stop. The limit on the number of trams available for service meant the operation was restricted to a ten-minute service. The trams were still most unusual vehicles to see on the streets of Wolverhampton and there were two minor traffic accidents. There was a portend when the ticket machines at several stops failed to operate. Staff acting as ambassadors guided customers on using the ticket machines. However, they soon found they had become tram conductors, selling tickets using duplicate pads. Where machines were working customers found that they did not accept notes. Passengers were not used to having to carry large quantities of coins to buy tickets. The difficulties were reported to the Italian manufacturers who sent engineers to investigate. They were appalled to find that the machines were out in the open, as they were designed for indoor operation only.

A newly delivered tram, believed to be 01, but without its number, black end bumpers, bogie side shrouds and front skirt is test run under power on a short length of the main line near the depot (seen in the background) on 30 April 1998. The car still has the original single blade windscreen wiper. Photo Roger Monk.

The official opening of the tramway took place on 14 November 1999. The Princess Royal visited the Midlands. Arriving in Wolverhampton, she boarded a tram and travelled to the depot. Here she unveiled a plaque commemorating her visit and the royal opening of the tramway. She then boarded the tram and rode to Snow Hill. Public service was suspended for the two hours the visit took. By this time revenue from ticket sales was dropping through the floor. Many stops had both ticket machines out of use and passengers would board without a ticket. If there was a member of staff on the tram selling tickets they would purchase one. But in most instances there was no one to buy a ticket from. In addition to those machines not issuing tickets there was a report of one that gave away "bucket loads of coins" when used.

Centro publish a 20 year strategy for transport outlining the proposals for expanding the Metro with three new lines to serve Halesowen, Walsall and Solihull (via the NEC and the airport). Centro also criticise Altram over its reliability of tram service. The target set by Centro was a reliability of 98.6%. In October, November and December 1999 it was 69%. Centro responded with a list of issues they had to deal with. These included being unable to use all its trams due to many being unserviceable. Car 03 was still out of action due to the lightning strike, others were waiting spares to repair faults. There were software problems and all over the system there was a high level of vandal damage including stones being thrown at trams smashing windows, meaning the tram had to be withdrawn from service on safety grounds. Though each stop had CCTV cameras to minimise vandal damage, four of the cameras had themselves been stolen. Ticket machines were still causing great problems, significantly reducing income.

During test running on 28 April 1999 25% of the Metro tram fleet are momentarily seen together at the Snow Hill terminus. Car 13 is arriving at the left hand platform, while car 09, on the right hand platform, waits to leave and occupy the single line section towards the St Pauls stop. Car 03 is parked at the far end of the left hand platform and car 10 is at the far end of the right hand platform (its pantograph is just visible behind car 09). Photo Roger Monk.

One of the early delivery of trams, un-numbered and carrying an Ansaldo poster, stands on the bridge over the Black Country New Road near the depot during a static test on 2 April 1998. Photo Roger Monk.

Tramcar number 08 arrives at Snow Hill Station with a crowd consisting of passengers leaving the tram and others waiting to board it. Customers waiting on the other platform appear to be content to wait for the next tram in order to get a seat.

CHAPTER 4

The Tramway Opens 1999 - 2000

The Railway Inspectorate approved the opening of the tramway on 13 May 1999. The tramway was formally opened a little later on 30 May. There was a short ceremony at the Snow Hill stop, where tramcar number 07 broke a celebratory tape. Mayors and civic dignitaries from the appropriate Councils rode the tramcar. As the tramcar moved across the different Council borders new tapes were broken. Then the first members of the public were able to ride on the trams. There was considerable attention from those interested in tramway transport. The first passenger to purchase a ticket was Philip Elverd, a member of the Tramway and Light Railway Society. He was quoted as saying "I was the first person to buy a ticket and am really going to enjoy this historic run."

The day did not go completely smoothly. Tramcar number 01 had an operational problem when its failsafe brake system operated without reason. The was another problem when vandals set fire to the Snow Hill escalator.

Tram number 14 at The Hawthorns stop on its way to Snow Hill.

The tramway started with a more limited service than had been hoped for, with a headway of a car every ten minutes in both directions. As detailed previously, tram number 03 was unserviceable after being struck by lightning on 28 May. In addition, tramcar 16 had not yet been commissioned. Nevertheless, the man-agement felt able to announce the introduction of a six-minute service after a few weeks. However, the service was dogged by relatively small problems, but ones that meant temporarily taking trams out of service and leaving gaps in the timetable.

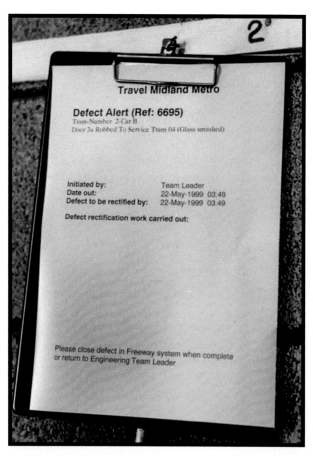

Travel Midland Metro

Defect Alert (Ref: 6695)
Tram-Number 2-Car B
Door 3a Robbed To Service Tram 04 (Glass smashed)

Initiated by: Team Leader
Date out: 22-May-1999 03:49
Defect to be rectified by: 22-May-1999 03:49

Defect rectification work carried out:

Please close defect in Freeway system when complete
or return to Engineering Team Leader

Notification in the depot showing that tram number 02 has had door 3A removed and fitted to tram number 04, as the glass in its door had been smashed.

The travelling time from one end of the route to the other was 35 minutes and the tramcars had a capacity of 158 (including 56 seated). Initially each tramcar was staffed only by a driver, passengers were required to purchase their tickets from machines at each stop.

Unfortunately, several problems became apparent with the operation of the tramway. The major issue for passengers was the high failure rate of door closures. Each door had a safety feature, so that the tram could not be driven off if any door was not fully closed. It was found that doors would often fail to close completely, stopping the tram from moving. As a temporary measure staff were allocated at stops to push the offending doors into the fully closed position to enable the tramcar to be driven to the next stop. Urgent work had to be undertaken to rectify the problem. However, the necessary spares from Italy were delayed. The more seriously unserviceable trams were used as sources of spare parts for other trams. Even with this provision many tramcars were not able to be placed back in service until the middle of January 2000.

To add to the difficulties the ticket machines were still causing major problems. As previously described the tramway had no conductors. Passengers were required to purchase their tickets at the stops prior to boarding the tram. The first difficulty that was encountered was the length of time this process took. When there were only one or two intending passengers it was not a problem, but at peak times with passengers desperate to get a ticket and board the tram, the delays created frustration and anger. Even those well acquainted with using the machines found them very slow and intensely annoying if a tram arrived and the passenger was third or fourth in a queue. As part of the introduction to the public, staff were allocated to the busiest stops to welcome customers and guide them on the use of the ticket machines. The situation got more difficult when ticket machines started failing. Apart from the terminal stops, each tram stop had two ticket machines, one for each platform. The tramway responded by saying the passengers would have to cross the line, use the machine on the other platform, purchase their ticket and return to their original platform. Not easy in the rush hour, and intensely annoying when the other ticket machine also did not work. The "Welcoming Staff" found themselves becoming ticket sellers, using duplicate pads. At one point it was said that half the machines were out of order at any one time and the tramway did not have sufficient staff to have ticket sellers at every stop. The dissatisfaction of passengers and the losses of revenue were immense. Maintenance staff started gluing scrappy notices on defective machines. "Out of service" was used, though the oddest

An all too frequent notice that passengers found on the ticket machines. Intensely annoying when both tickets machines at a stop were out of action. This led to a significant drop in revenue.

had to be "Press E for code F". An added complication was that the ticket machines did not take notes, only coins. Intending passengers had to ensure that they had enough coins to pay for a fare. It was said that the tramway management contacted the manufacturers to ask them to come to Britain to check their machines. On arriving the machine management took one look and said, "But they are outside, we built them for use inside ticket offices." To add to the difficulties there were problems with vandals. The ticket machines were seen by some as large moneyboxes and as such attracted undesirable attention. While the cash in the machines was well protected the thieves still had a success rate of around 75% making the theft very tempting. Such attempts to remove money from the machines usually relied on brute force, which damaged the machine in the process. The tramway was forced to create a team of trouble shooters who spent their time identifying broken machines and repairing them.

In order to obtain Government funding the number of tramcars had been pared back to the absolute minimum. The initial proposal by the Government was for the tramway to have just one spare above the number required for a full six-minute service. The operators were concerned that this was insufficient and paid for an extra tramcar (number 16). Other teething problems added to the pressure on the tramway and it was realised that a six-minute service was a difficult goal. An example was the discovery that the centre bogies of the tramcars were prone to derailing at point-work, due to the incorrect profile of the wheels. The solution was to reprofile all the wheels. However, a cost saving move at the design stage was to not have a wheel profiling lathe. In consequence the bogies had to be taken by road to the Tysley Depot of British Rail where they had such a facility. At one stage the number of serviceable trams dropped to eight, meaning half the fleet were unavailable for service. However, on a happier note door problems were getting less.

The tramway infrastructure and rolling stock were owned by Transport for West Midlands initially, except for tram number 16, seen here at The Hawthorns. This was purchased and owned by the operators, Altram Consortia, as they considered that the fleet funded by the Government was insufficient to maintain service reliability. When the consortia split up number 16 was passed to the owners of the tramway.

Cars 05, 11 and 15 in the sidings at the Potters Lane depot, Wednesbury.

The six-minute service was an aspiration but attempts to run such a frequency proved very difficult as the failure rate was such that trams had to be taken out of service, leaving gaps and frustrated passengers. In fact, it was not until July 2000 that reliability improved enough for the tramway to announce a revised time-table that had trams running every six to seven minutes between 7.00am and 7.00pm (before 7.00am and after 7.00pm the frequency was every ten minutes).

The combination of machine breakdown and vandalism significantly reduced the income of the tramway. The Management decided to abandon the ticket machines and instead employ conductors (or as the tramway called them "Customer Service Representatives", CSRs) that were recruited to collect fares. The amount of fare dodging dropped dramatically, and a beneficial side effect was that passengers said that they felt safer travelling on a tram with a CSR. In line with Government policy for public railed transport the operator of the system was responsible for hiring and paying for the system to be policed. The contract was advertised, and the winning police force was British Transport Police. BTP had much experience of operations on the railway, but this was the first contract they had with a tramway system.

The trials and tribulations of the Tramway Management were far from over. Centro, as the "purchaser" of the tramway, was not happy with the performance of the operator. The standard required was a reliability of 98.6%. In the last three months of 1999 it was 69%. As has been mentioned the numbers of trams that were waiting for spare parts was a significant problem.

During the millennium there were large numbers of celebratory events where the public relied on public transport, including the trams, to get to and from events. However, in addition to all the other problems, the ticket machines stopped working at 2300 hours. For the millennium the tramway employed CSRs for the service that ran until 04.00. They sold special £3.00 tickets to ensure that the tramway received its revenue during the celebrations. The initiative was a great success and led to the introduction of CSRs on normal services.

However, there was a plus side. A survey of passengers found that 65% of passengers were regular users, 80% rated the service good or very good and the vehicles good or very good. 70% rated security as good or very good. 71% rated the announcements as good or very good, 15% of morning peak passengers had transferred from using cars, while 35% had a car available for the journey they made.

The Metro Centre

Opened by

HRH The Princess Royal

14th September 1999

Above: The inscription on the plaque.

The Princess Royal about to unveil the plaque commemorating her official opening of the Midland Metro. A black and white photo for "Tramfare".

It was nearly six months after the start of public operation that the tramway was officially opened. The opening ceremony was undertaken by the Princess Royal on 14 September. I was fortunate in having been given an invitation to represent "Tramfare", the magazine of the Tramway and Light Railway Society. The Princess Royal arrived at Wolverhampton St Georges to board a special tram that took her and representatives of the Tramway and Local Authorities to the depot at Wednesbury. Here she disembarked and walked down the steps leading to the depot. A stand had been erected in the entrance to the repair shops on which a plaque was mounted that was inscribed with the words; "The Metro Centre Opened by HRH The Princess Royal 14th September 1999". After a short time chatting to staff at the depot and posing for the press photographers, she returned to the tram stop and boarded her tramcar to travel the rest of the line to Birmingham Snow Hill.

The royal blessing to the Metro gave the local Councillors a boost and they were soon proclaiming that by 2005 there would be two new branches, one to Five Ways and the other to Merry Hill shopping centre. These were to be followed by lines to Quinton or Halesowen and others to Solihull and the NEC and the airport.

The Princess Royal, having unveiled the plaque commemorating the formal opening of the depot, boarded a tram at Wednesbury stop to ride to Snow Hill. A black and white photo for Tramfare.

There was a far more serious incident on 29 December 1999 at the level crossing on Swan Lane, near the Black Lake tram stop. A motorist ignored a red traffic light and drove his vehicle over the tramway just as a tramcar reached the crossing. Unfortunately, the passenger in the car was killed in the collision. There was a second collision on 6 March 2000, again between a motorcar and a tramcar, luckily without fatalities. The tramcars were a new form of transport and car drivers in the area were not used to meeting anything on what they thought was a still an abandoned railway line. All the tram drivers were informed of the accidents and were instructed to take special care when approaching the crossing and to proceed over it very slowly.

The most distinctive structure on the metro is the "Wishbone" bridge on the approach to the St Paul's terminus in Wolverhampton.

Tramcars 05 and 07 running along the Bilston Road, Wolverhampton during driver training.

A line up of trams during the testing period. 02 and an unnumbered car are on the main running lines while car 04 is on the spur leading to the depot. The area in and around the depot is well protected by CCTV cameras on masts, three of which are seen in this photo.

In the winter of 2000/2001 there was a difficulty with the overhead wiring. All the reserved track is equipped with a double wire overhead for each track. However, the street section in Wolverhampton was built with a single wire. In common with all modern tramways the path of the wire zig-zagged along the route. This was to ensure that there is an even amount of wear along the length of the pantograph contact strip. By necessity the wire is exposed to the elements and it was found that during very cold and wet winter nights the overhead wire was prone to icing up and this caused problems with the first few trams of the day. To prevent this happening one of the trams would be run at intervals through the night scraping the ice off the wire. Inevitably this procedure was known as the ghost tram. In the winter of 2000/2001 there was an unexpected very cold night in February. This meant that the while the service trams were running the overhead wiring was heated up by the electric current. However, when the service ended for the day no arrangements had been made for the ghost tram. Water had accumulated on the overhead wires and when the tram service stopped this water froze, this particularly affected the street section with its single wire overhead. The disruption to the first service cars of the morning meant that checking the weather forecast became a priority.

The initial impact of the tramway was disappointing. It had been predicted that passenger numbers would be between 14 and 20 million passengers a year. For the year 1999/2000 the actual number was 4.8 million. The tramway management were anticipating an increase over the next few years to get closer to the forecast numbers. In fact the rise peaked at 8 million for the years 2019-2020 and 2020-2021 prior to the impact of Coronavirus.

Note the section of interlaced track used in order that the point blades are located on the reserved section of track away from other road vehicles to minimise the risk of damage by lorries crossing the rails. The rails show that the second platform was rarely used and it was later taken out of service and the rails to that platform were lifted.

CHAPTER 5

A Difficult Beginning to the Millennium 2001 - 2010

Once the Millennium celebrations were over, the Midlands Metro looked forward to settling down and building up its passenger numbers. The senior management were resolving the ticket machine issues. Car 03 was still out of service and car 07 was waiting for spares following being struck by lightning during the previous year. Then another unexpected challenge arose. The system began to have problems with the insulators separating the sections of the overhead wire. An insulator near West Bromwich Central blew up allowing the live wire to drop to the ground. The tram service halted on 26 June 2001. The Railway Inspectorate carried out an investigation and reported that the design of the insulator was faulty. They decided that the road running section in Wolverhampton was particularly hazardous. Operation between Priestfield and St Georges was banned from 4 July 2001 until repairs had been undertaken, because of fears that, if an insulator on that section had exploded, a live 750V overhead wire could fall to the road and endanger the public. The tramway immediately implemented a programme to replace all insulators at night when trams were not running and placed speed limits on vulnerable sections. At a meeting on 6 July with the Railway Inspectorate the rectification programme was put forward and it was agreed that all tramway operations could recommence while the insulators were being replaced.

The anticipated rise in passenger numbers failed to materialise. The numbers of passengers were holding steady at around five million a year, well short of the anticipated 14 to 20 million a year. This shortfall and the cost of addressing the technical problems meant that the tramway ran a loss of £4 million during its first eighteen months of operation. Phil Bateman, spokesman for Travel Midland Metro, said: "We are in a better position now in terms of reliability and we are seeing passengers approval of the system continuing to grow. We have had more than our fair share of vandalism and we have had setbacks, but it was a new system and there are always difficulties on any new company. The important thing is that we are still in operation and the people of the West Midlands like the system. They have seen its reliability grow." A spokesperson from Centro said that two additional routes were planned one from Wednesbury to Merry Hill and Brierley Hill, the other an extension in central Birmingham.

Midland Metro suggested to Altram that some of the tramcars could be named after famous West Midland people. The idea was accepted and tram 01 (later transferred to tram 04) was named after the Coventry born inventor of the jet engine. Despite only being a few years old the tram is showing signs of corrosion.

In 2001, as the agency responsible for monitoring the operation of the tramway, Midland Metro put forward a plan to name some of the tramcars after famous West Midland personalities. They put the idea to Al-tram, who said they had no objection, but did not want to get involved in choosing the names.

Tram 06 carries the name of Alan Garner who was a City Councillor for Wolverhampton and Vice Chair of West Midlands Passenger Transport Authority when the Metro was being developed.

An errant lorry collided with one of the piers of the tramway bridge at Great Bridge Road, Wednesbury, in May and, for safety, the tramway placed a temporary speed limit on tramcars crossing it. There was another problem on 26 June 2001 when the section between Birmingham and Black Lake suffered a power outage for 30 hours. Travel West Midlands introduced random drug and alcohol tests for the drivers of buses and trams. A spokesman said there was not a huge problem, but felt they needed a policy in place to ensure the safety of passengers and staff.

The West Midlands PTA approved the preparation of a Transport and Works Order to build an extension of the tramway to Brierley Hill via Merry Hill estimated at £114 million and an extension from Snow Hill to Five Ways and then the Edgbaston Shopping Centre at £51 million, which would incorporate an 8% grade which was above the specification of their current fleet of tramcars. The target was to get an Act approved by Spring 2002. However, soon after the decision to go ahead, Railtrack was placed into administration, which affected the proposals as the Brierley Hill extension relied on using existing heavy rail trackwork. On a good note, reliability took a turn for the better during December 2001 with only one incident (due to an obstruction on the overhead between St Georges and Priestfield requiring a bus substitution service for a few hours).

The year 2002 started with Midland Metro having rectified the issues with the overhead wire insulators. All the defective components had been replaced and the temporary speed limits removed. At this time, there were twelve tramcars available for service. Ticket machines had been removed from all stops except Snow Hill, St Georges, Bilston and Wednesbury. Using Customer Service Representatives (CSRs) had dramatically reduced the number of passengers travelling without tickets. There were more CCTV installations at the stops. Less welcome to travellers was the announcement that fares were increasing on 6 January 2002. Meanwhile a Committee from Coventry Council visited Nancy to examine the guided trolleybus system. They commented that they were impressed by the system. To their embarrassment it closed a month later in March on safety grounds.

Early in 2002 the Midland Metro General Manager gave a frank report of the condition of the Tramway. He told Councillors that the tramcars were "crap" and fundamentally defective with wiring like "plates of spaghetti". Rather than a fleet of similar tramcars, each had a different type of electrical wiring. Of the 16 cars in the fleet three had been long term out of service due to the delays in availability of spares being sent from Naples. Ridership had fallen short of the 9 million passengers a year forecast, being just 6 million passengers a year. The contract specified a headway of six minutes, in operation it was advertised as eight minutes and in reality it was ten minutes. Ansaldo and Centro reacted against these comments.

Ansaldo said it was up to the purchaser to quality control the production. A Centro spokesman responded by saying it thought it was dealing with professional organisations, then added that the Government had not helped by insisting the line was built "on the cheap" and placing the highest priority on the requirement that the line be handed over to the private sector. He also criticised the proposed city centre extension which in his view contained inherent problems that would make operation very difficult and that running up Pinfold Street was crazy.

On a lighter note the Tramway had a most unusual passenger in the early part of the year. The tramway had been called by a member of the public to tell them that a goat was wandering about the tramway track and was in danger of being knocked down. Drivers were told to take care driving in that section, and one stopped and managed to persuade the goat to enter the tram. It was given a ride from Black Lake to Great Western Street stop and taken to the depot. The RSPCA was called to take care of it. The owners were found who said that a gate had been left open by refuse collectors and the goat had wandered off. This is the only known example of livestock being carried by a modern British tram.

The need to regularly reprofile wheels and the lack of a wheel lathe, meant that trams had to be taken out of service for protracted periods. To overcome this the tramway purchased a wheel lathe and was able to significantly reduce the length of time that trams were out of service. However, over the year fare income failed to break even with costs. In its first eighteen months of operation the system lost £3.7 million. However, Phil Bateman stated that operational losses were now "a thing of the past"

By April 2002, the tramway was in a better situation. It was able to keep twelve trams in service and provide an eight minute headway during the day and twelve minutes off-peak. It was even able to have a spare tramcar, making thirteen available cars. The Management were aiming to increase the number of available cars to fourteen, but the old bugbear of lack of spares prevented this. The replacement schedule for the 1,100 defective insulators was going ahead with around 80% having been replaced. Recruitment and training of CSRs was complete, and all cars now carried a driver and a CSR.

An article was published, written by Centro's Transport Planning Team Leader and the Principal Project Manager Metro, suggesting that the city should explore the initiative of the tramway and railway in Karlsruhe where the street tramway shares a line with the local railway. They suggested exploring sharing track with the main line railway. The passenger numbers using the Metro were once again disappointing with the annual figures for 1999-2000 being just 4.8 million; 2000/2001 5.4 million; and 2001/2002 4.8 million. The reaction by the West Midlands was to ask the Government for a bigger slice of future funding to enable better integration of the bus, train, car, and metro provision.

The approach to Wolverhampton puts the tram on the road, in amongst other traffic. Like all vehicles on the road the trams must obey all traffic lights.

Tramcars 01, 09 and another outside the depot building, taken before the tramway opened to the public.

The year 2003 did not start well. In February, the driver of a car died after his vehicle was in collision with a tramcar on 9 February. The accident happened on a level crossing near the car park at Priestfield Station. The year saw another fatality on the tramway that was the subject of a Coroner's Enquiry. A 30-year-old woman was hit by a tram and died on 12 December 2003. The tram driver told the Coroner that it was 11pm on a winter night when he had seen an object on the track but thought his tram would clear it. However, he heard a thud as his tram passed over it.

On the whole, the year 2003 was less fraught for the Tramway. By then the system had removed all the ticket machines and CSRs were collecting fares on all tramcars. The reliability of tramcars was better, though there were still issues regarding the supply of spares from Italy. There were proposals for a road running extension in Birmingham City centre, however some suggested that the Tramway should be fenced off to protect pedestrians. The Council responded by saying they were not in favour of fences. Vandals were continuing to cause problems including pushing a motor car down an embankment in Hill Top, blocking the tram line. To prevent any recurrences a security fence was installed.

A survey of passengers in 2003 found that 95% were in favour of extensions to the Tramway. However, the members of Birmingham City Council disagreed among themselves as to which mode of transport would be best for the city. Suggestions included an underground railway, a trolleybus system, extending the bus network, discouraging car use and building a monorail, while Dudley Council suggested that the existing Stourbridge to Brierley Hill railway line could have a Metro service running alongside it. Independent opinion was that these arguments would persuade the Government not to fund any extension. This opinion was strengthened by comments from the Transport Minister that the extension proposals were considered unrealistic and too costly. In his view using low cost buses was the answer.

The response of the former Director General of Centro (1987-1998) was to say "The Region's Politicians had destroyed hard won legal powers for short-termism. The plans are a terrible mess with his successors moving from a broad vision to a narrow one." He added "The Birmingham City Council had divested themselves of powers to build that had taken eight years to acquire. "

In December there was a Public Enquiry into the planned expansion of the Birmingham City extension. The Centro Project Director gave evidence that the extension was key to the development of Birmingham as a world class city. Oppositions to the extension included the Hyatt, Novotel and Burlington Hotels; House of Fraser and Beatties; Calthorpe Estate and Kestral properties; and the Victorian Society.

One ray of sunshine was the news that ridership had increased by 5.2% to 5 million passengers per year. Andrew Steel announced that he would be retiring from his role as General Manager of Travel West Midlands. In April 2004, the Government announced its decisions on the Metro expansion proposals. There were now new "value for money" criteria, particularly that they now required a cost benefit ratio of 1:5 (from the previous 1:3). Only the extension to Quinton via Five Ways and that from the city centre to Great Barr met this condition. The proposed line to the airport and that to Walsall from Wolverhampton failed to meet the new criteria.

In June 2004, the Conservative Councillors put forward a proposal to build a £200 million underground system for Birmingham. This would effectively stop any further development of the light rail system in the city. Centro were worried that this proposal would mean that Central Government would refuse to fund extension of the Metro until there was agreement on the future of public transport in the city. The Council had estimated the cost of such an underground as £200 million, while Centro said that the cost would be nearer £3 billion and that any delay in the planned expansion would last for at least ten years.

On 17 July tram number 10 was named "John Stanley Webb", a noted local tramway historian. This brought the number of named trams to six. The others were Ray Lewis (number 03); Sister Dora (05); Alan Garner (06); Jeff Astle (09); and Theresa Stewart (11).

Tramcar number 08 was another tram to be named. It received the name "Joseph Chamberlain" after the Birmingham industrialist and politician.

Local Council elections were held on 10 June 2004 resulting in a hung Birmingham Council with 53 Labour, 39 Conservative and 28 Liberal members. Despite not having a majority the Conservatives contin-ued to push for an underground railway and sought agreement for funding a feasibility study at a cost of £100,000. The other parties complained that they were being held to ransom. The two main parties agreed that they would share the positions of Chair and Vice Chair of the West Midlands Passenger Transport Authority (which was to consist of 13 Conservatives, 12 Labour and 2 Liberal

The Metro announced it had 100% reliability during the summer. However, it was not clear what the service levels were being measured against, not the originally contracted six-minute service, possibly the eight-minute service or even the ten-minute service. However, passenger numbers continued at the increased level of 5.1 million per annum with thirteen tramcars available for service. The tramway also attended to a weed problem on the reserved track sections. A weed killer vehicle was hired to spray the track-bed at night.

Tramcar number 11 approaching Bradley Lane stop on driver training duties.

September saw a fire that damaged lineside cables at Priestfield. This shut the whole system down for a while. After some hours, a service was resumed between Birmingham and Wednesbury, but it took six days before the service could operate over the whole route. A ten-minute headway was worked until December when the eight-minute schedule was resumed. As a sales initiative the tramway sent information to every firm in Birmingham that they could make savings for every member of staff by issuing them with an annual £700 tramway pass, saving the cost of an off road car parking place of £1,700. Birmingham Conservative Councillors were still pressing for a feasibility study (now costing £150,000) for an underground system for Birmingham. Centro commented that Birmingham Council were mistaken in promoting an underground railway for the city. The Transport Secretary stepped into the argument and warned the City Council and the West Midlands PTA about the proposed underground railway. He told them that the Government was not keen on the plan and dropped hints that arguments between the PTA and the Council would just delay any development.

The tramway also suffered more vandalism. On 20 November vandals had dumped a pair of metal gates across the track at Bilston stop and had also thrown a noose over the overhead line. The tramway commented that the perpetrators were lucky not to have been electrocuted. November also saw delays in the Priestfield area, first by a failure of traffic signals on the approach to St Georges and a second when tram 13 collided with a lorry carrying gas cylinders on Bilston Road. The tram pushed the lorry into three other vehicles, as well as damaging the tramcar.

Early in 2005 the Tramway published details of the proposed route from Wolverhampton to Walsall. The cost was said to be £300 million with 2013 as the expected opening date. The route would need an extra 27 new trams to provide the service. The proposed route from Wednesbury to Brierley Hill was also an-nounced and the forecast cost was £139 million. Despite the strong reservations of the Transport Secre-tary, some Birmingham Councillors were still promoting an underground railway.

In 2005 the Merry Hill shopping centre had a new owner, who promised £35 million funding to ensure that the proposed branch from Wednesbury would reach the shopping complex. The anticipated opening date was 2013. There was another naming ceremony when tramcar 08 was given the name Joseph Chamber-lain. The tramway had some good news in July, the Government had taken on the recommendation of the inspector leading the public enquiry and gave their approval to the proposed city centre extension to New Street Station.

The City Council receive the Consultant's report they had commissioned on the viability of a city centre underground railway. The report concluded that street tramways were more financially attractive than an underground railway. They did add that an underground might be feasible in the long term, but currently they would recommend trams. The City Council had spent £300,000 on the consultant's report (initially estimated at £100,000) and now said that they were totally behind the Midland Metro. The recently appointed President of the Chamber of Commerce entered the argument with the suggestion to build a monorail system. The example that he quoted was the monorail at Disney World, seemingly not understanding the different demands on a public transport system joining two major cities and a theme park ride.

More tramcars received names in 2005/6. Number 04 became "Sir Frank Whittle" to recognise the inventor of the jet engine who was born in Coventry. Number 13 was given the name "Anthony Nolan" to honour the boy whose mother set up the world's first bone marrow register to match donors with people needing a transplant. Number 14 was named after "Jim Eaves" (Eric James Eaves) who was a long serving Birmingham City Councillor and Lord Mayor of the city for 1974-1975, he was also an Honorary Alderman and a magistrate. Number 15 was given the name "Agenoria" the name of the oldest preserved steam railway locomotive (currently on display at the National Railway Museum York). It was built in Stourbridge and worked in the Black Country.

Tram number 15 was named "Agenoria" after a preserved steam railway locomotive.

At the end of 2005 Councillors approved the replacement of the fleet of 16 tramcars. They were only six years old, but their specification meant that they would not be able to climb the hill of Pinfold Street on the westward extension. The Metro management were pleased that during 2005 the number of crimes against the Metro dropped by 22.6%. There was disappointment in July when the Government announced it would not be funding Metro's extension plans. In an alternative move the Metro made an application to the Transport Innovation Fund that had been set up in 2004.

Early in August the system was disrupted when it had technical problems with the power supply. The whole service ceased at 21.00 on Friday 4 August and ran a skeleton service on Saturday 5 August. There was a boost for the Metro management when independent experts said that the £430 million extensions represented value for money. This was reinforced when the Black Country Authorities announced that the expansion of the network was vital to the future of industry over the whole of the Black Country. They said that £200 million a year and 40,000 jobs would be lost without the expansion because there would be an increase in road congestion.

Another problem emerged on the tramway. The passenger information system at tram stops started failing. Half the information screens had ceased operating while many of the others were giving incorrect information. At Snow Hill stop the escalators stopped working and passengers leaving the platform were faced with either a stiff climb up the stairway or queueing for the lift.

In 2006 two of the partners owning Altram decide to leave the joint venture owing to the losses being incurred. West Midlands Travel Limited acquired the Altram shares held by Ansaldo Transporti Sistemi Ferroviari SpA and Laing Infrastructure Holdings Limited. Operation of the Tramway now rested entirely with West Midlands Travel (trading as Travel West Midlands). It was a wholly owned subsidiary of National Express Group plc. The system was renamed "National Express Midland Metro".

An unusual incident occurred on 26 April when a member of the public fell in front of a tram at the Handsworth Booth Street stop. He had been given a lift in a police car to the tram stop after the Police Officers had met him in Smethwick. After dropping him off he had fallen on the line in front of an oncoming tramcar and became trapped under the tram. After being taken to the hospital, he was found to have life threatening injuries.

There was another accident a month and a half later, on 8 June 2006. A tramcar (06) was in collision with a taxi on the New Swan Lane level crossing. The force of the impact pushed the taxi across the junction where it collided with a stationery lorry. The driver and the passenger of the taxi were taken to hospital and discharged two hours later. No other persons were hurt. The tram driver had approached the crossing with his signal at stop. He anticipated it would change to proceed and failed to slow down with the result that it collided with the taxi. As the driver of the tram was unused to operating the emergency brake, he did not do so. The matter was investigated by the Rail Accident Investigation Branch that recommended that the initial training programme and refresher programmes should ensure familiarity of the operation of the hazard brake. Management was informed that they should not discourage the use of the hazard brake.

Car 14 at The Hawthorns tram stop for the West Bromwich Albion football ground.

On 19 December tramcars 09 and 10 collided while both travelled in the same direction in Soho. Services to Snow Hill were disrupted for seven hours. The Rail Accident Investigation Branch were informed, and they carried out an investigation. They found that tram 09 had stopped due to a technical fault. Tram 10 had caught up tram 09, but the driver of tram 10 had been temporarily blinded by a low-lying sun. He had failed to see tram 09 and collided with it. Thirteen passengers were taken to hospital and all were discharged later the same day. The driver had deployed the sun blind to enable him to see ahead, however, there was a problem with the blind which caused him to remove his hand from the controller and look upwards. The blind continued to cause a problem and, when the driver looked forward, he saw tram 09 stationery in front of him. Applying the emergency brake, his tramcar struck the rear of tram 09. The driver of 09 was talking to the Control Centre when the collision occurred, so he was able to immediately report it. The recommendations of the RAIB were that tram sun blinds should be modified so that they remained down when deployed and that their operation should be regularly checked. Procedures were also changed to require hazard lights to be used whenever a tramcar was causing an obstruction. Finally, it was recommended that a risk assessment should be carried out to identify the appropriate response to unexpected hazards. The immediate effect of the accident was to remove two tramcars from service.

With a scheduled six to ten minute interval between cars it is unusual to see two trams close together on the same track.

At the end of 2006 the Metro received more disappointing news. The Transport Minister told the Metro that he would not be making decisions regarding the funding application to the Transport Innovation Fund until all the bids had been received and evaluated in 2008. Birmingham Council suggested making a daily £5 congestion charge for cars entering Birmingham. This was opposed by the Chamber of Commerce who commented that such a charge should only be made after public transport in the city was improved.

An unusual event happened on 8 November when a motorist managed to drive his Mercedes C Class coupé onto the reserved Metro track near the Snow Hill stop. The driver was arrested on suspicion of drink driving. It took over five hours to remove the car, during which time services terminated at St Paul's.

The new year 2007 saw Centro (the West Midlands PTE) bringing in a new branding for all the tram, bus and train services in its area. These were now to be known as "Network West Midlands". The misfortunes of the tramway continued in the new year. On 27 January 2007 a tram collided with a car, putting the tram out of action for several days while it was repaired. Just two days later, on the 29th tram 06 derailed on the points at the Snow Hill stop. Service trams had to terminate at St Paul's while the tram was re-railed. This was the subject of a Rail Accident Investigation Branch report that concluded that the accident was caused by incorrect repair to the switch blade. The point was repaired and procedures were changed to ensure that future repairs were to correct standards.

Construction of a new ramp and bridge to take the Metro alongside Snow Hill Station up to Bull Street. The opening of the street running section in the city centre saw the Snow Hill Station stop closed and replaced by St Chads stop, located at this end of the station.

In the middle of 2007 work started on building a new £9 million viaduct alongside Snow Hill Station to take the Metro line along the east side of the railway station. This would allow the building of the extension into the city centre and release platform 4 for railway services.

At the same time tram 12 was given an internal change. Seating was relocated to give more space for wheelchair users. A programme of similar modifications was planned for the rest of the fleet, starting with trams 09 and 10. During the modifications the livery was changed with the trams being repainted in magenta and silver with blue doors. This reflected the change in ownership from Altram to West Midlands Travel. The number of CCTV cameras at stops was being increased from 72 to 175. This coincided with a refurbishment of the public address system.

Later in the year there was another hold up, this time at The Royal stop. During repairs to points at a crossover a point motor was damaged when it was accidentally dropped. There were delays in obtaining a replacement which prevented trams turning short at the Royal, instead they had to halt at an earlier stop, Priestfield, leaving passengers with a 20 minute bus ride to the city centre instead of a short walk. A spokesman for the Metro said that the mechanism had become damaged during an engineering inspection but that the situation should be resolved within a week.

Centro suggested that the planned extension to Brierley Hill could be funded using money generated by a congestion charge scheme. However, there was little support for this measure by the local authorities and as a result the Department of Transport reject the proposals. As an entertainment for travellers The Haw-thorne tram stop put on an image and light show during November and December. Despite such innovative projects, ridership on the Metro fell again. In 2006/7 the number of passengers dropped to 4.9 million, down 6% on the previous year. The fall was blamed on service closures because of vandalism.

The Blackpool tramway had hired a rail grinding machine during the winter of 2007/8. It was now hired by Midland Metro to remove corrugations on the rails between Priestfield and St Georges. Despite the Government having doubts about the two extensions to the system, Metro management continued with their plans for improvements.

Tramcar number 07 made a reappearance in service eight years after its crash. It had been repainted in the "Network West Midlands" magenta and silver livery. Following the decision of the West Midlands Council not to introduce congestion charging to fund the tramway expansions, the tramway initiated an investigation to explore other options for funding the work. The projects needed £2 million funding.

Car number 07, resplendent in its new magenta and silver livery stands next to car 16 at The Hawthorns stop.

Later in the year the service was stopped between Snow Hill and Wednesbury Parkway to allow the replacement of rails in Hill Top tunnel and the erection of new overhead wiring at Winson Green. During the work the tramway operated a fifteen-minute headway between Wolverhampton and Wednesbury Parkway. Wolverhampton Council said it would like the tramway to be extended to Tettenhall, Penn and along the A449. In the latter part of 2008 Centro started the process with the aim of replacing the existing fleet by 2012. It planned that the new trams would run not only on the existing route but also on the two extensions. £10 million funding was expected in the next few years from a new housing tariff. Merry Hill would also fund £36 million and Centro £49.5 million with £290 million still to find.

The Transport and Works Act Order for Wolverhampton City Centre loop was being drafted. The proposal was to go from St Georges, along Princess Street, Lichfield Street and Pipers Row with a spur from Lichfield Street to the railway station and Sun Street. The fall in the number of passengers carried in the year 2006/7 (dropping from 5.2 million to 4.9 million) was attributed to service closures because of vandalism. It was said that approval for the extensions would only be given if the ridership rose to 5.8 million a year.

The year 2008 ended with Birmingham City Council being criticised by local media for not backing the Metro extension from city centre to Five Ways. Seeking funding for the expansion of the network, Centro PTE (made up of seven local authorities) believed that money from business rates could be used to release £500 million for rail, tram and bus services. Meanwhile West Midlands PTA bought land needed for the Brierley Hill extension. However, Centro had allowed the powers to build the line to lapse in 1990s and needed to be applied for authority again.

2008/9 saw a small increase in ridership with passenger numbers going up from 4.9 million to 5 million. Two old ideas re-emerged despite having been shown to be non-starters. They were an underground for Birmingham and the use of tram-trains. The idea of a monorail was mooted (again) to run between the city centre and the airport. It was agreed that the proposal for an extension to Brierley Hill would be delayed until after 2014. Instead the priority should be to extend the current route at both ends (to Five Ways and closer to Wolverhampton centre). This would bring the cost down to £60 million. The highest priority was to replace the existing 16 trams with 25 new trams. Optimistically passenger numbers were expected to rise from 5 million to 8 million as a result of the changes.

Like many public bodies, Centro invested money not immediately needed into short term loans to banks. The Icelandic Bank offered attractive rates and Centro deposited not immediately required funds with it. Unfortunately, the Icelandic Bank failed, and investors lost their money. Centro was estimated to have lost £800,000.

Tram 13 is parked at the end of Snow Hill platform, having had a mechanical failure. When the opportunity arises it will be towed back to the depot for repairs.

In April, an over-height articulated lorry attempted to drive under the Midland Metro bridge on Great Bridge Road (on the border between Tipton and Bilston). It struck the bridge and got stuck. Police closed the road and firefighters worked to free the vehicle so that it could be towed away. Although there were large signs warning drivers of the limited height, there was a history of tall vehicles striking the bridge. There had been twenty such incidents in the previous six years. As a precaution, trams passing over the bridge were required to slow down to reduce the strain on the bridge.

In 2010 there was a major programme of renewal. The tramway had to be closed for two separate weeks while overhead wires were renewed at a cost of £430,000 and the control and communications systems overhauled, costing £530,000. This was a major disruption for the 14,000 passengers using the tramway every day. The first closure took place in October of 2010 between Snow Hill and Black Lake and the second occurred between 17 and 20 April 2011 between Wolverhampton, St Georges and Wednesbury Park-way.

The Government gave approval for the Birmingham City Centre extension to New Street Station. In May 2010, the Transport Minister visited the Metro and confirmed a grant of £127 million to build the city centre link from Snow Hill Station to New Street Station. In August the new Conservative-Liberal coalition called a halt on the expansion and delayed the decision until the Autumn. However, where contracts had been approved (advance works, purchase of new trams, smartcards, the Wolverhampton interchange and New Street reconstruction) work was allowed go ahead. The extension to New Street Station was approved in November. The £127 million funding includes the fleet of new trams, and a new workshop and maintenance facility at Wednesbury.

There was a positive change as the number of passengers carried in 2010/11 showed an increase of 100,000 over the previous year. It was believed this was due to the rise in fuel prices, making travelling to work by car less attractive. However, the total number of passengers carried in the year (4.8 million) was still well short of the target of 8 million.

The battery operated depot shunter, used to move trams around where there are no overhead wires.

The Snow Hill Station tram stop that opened in 1999 and closed in 2015 when the line was extended to run alongside the Station to link with New Street Station and go on to Edgbaston.

In 2013 tram number 11 was given a unique colour scheme based on the original Birmingham Corporation Tramways livery. It marked the 60th anniversary of the final tram to run in the streets of the city. Here it is seen at Wednesbury Parkway. It had its nameplate "Theresa Stewart" removed for the repaint and it is yet to be replaced.

CHAPTER 6

Planning for the Future 2011 - 2015

The year 2011 did not have a good start for the Tramway as the proposal, backed by the West Midlands Passenger Transport Executive Centro and other local authorities, to share the use of the Wednesbury to Brierley Hill freight railway line was described as "unrealistic" by the Planning Inspector, who reported that "it is not currently practical or viable to also introduce passenger rail services on this line and therefore unrealistic for the joint core strategy to include this long-term aspiration in its transport proposals for the plan period, no matter how desirable." This was a blow as the route was key to development of the Tramway.

West Midlands Passenger Transport Executive Centro had ambitions for other expansions for the tram-way and had submitted proposals to the Government. These were to extend the tramway from Snow Hill Station to link with New Street Station (to coincide with the rebuilding of the station) and later go on to Edgbaston; to renew the fleet of tramcars; and to build a new maintenance depot at Wednesbury. There was good news at the beginning of the year when the Government approved funding of £75 million (the schemes cost £129 million). Originally the expectation was that passenger numbers would climb to 14 to 20 million. They had remained steady at around 5 million. It was expected that an extra 3.5 million passengers per annum would use the extension.

The Metro track at the entrance to Snow Hill Station. The extension of line 1 would leave the existing route before the track entered the station and go over the brambles to a bridge, yet to be built, then run along the outside of the station building.

The very slow availability of spare parts had soon become evident after the Tramway opened and proved a major problem. It was made more of an issue in 2000 when tram number 07 had a major accident requiring the replacement of many parts. While it was parked in the depot waiting for the parts it was used as a source of spare parts for other tramcars. After a few years the required spares arrived, and it was put back in service. At this time tram number 01 was withdrawn as it needed spares from Italy. Number 01 now became the source of spares. This was soon followed by tramcar number 02 that needed specialist parts only obtainable from Italy, but as AnsaldoBreda did not keep a stock of spares all the parts had to be manufactured. By April 2011 both trams numbers 01 and 02 were stuck in the depot, slowly having various parts removed to give to other trams. This arrangement meant that the donating tramcars became known as "Christmas Trees" as they gave presents to the other trams.

Unfortunately, early in the afternoon of 20 April 2011, the Tramway suffered a significant accident when the overhead line collapsed. Tramcar number 13, heading to Birmingham, was nearing the Jewellery Quarter tram stop when its pantograph struck a cantilever bracket, part of the overhead line, and pulled down 200 metres of overhead wire and equipment. Components from the overhead fell and struck the tramcar shattering the glass in the front and rear windscreens, the driver's cab side window and another window in the passenger compartment, causing injuries to the driver and six passengers. The driver brought the tram to a stop at the Jewellery Quarter platform where the twenty passengers were able to exit the tram. Those that were injured were taken to hospital for treatment. The RAIB were informed and an investigation was held. Recommendations were made regarding inspection of the overhead and staff training. The immedi-ate consequences of the accident were to close the line between the Jewellery Quarter and Soho Benson Road tram stops while repairs to the overhead took place. Tram 13 was severely damaged and had to be towed back to the depot. From 24 April 2011 a limited service was able to be resumed which became a full service on 28 April 2011.

In July tenders for new trams were invited from Alstom, Bombardier, CAF, Siemens and Stadler. The order was to be placed in 2012 and delivery by mid-2014. In February 2012 an announcement was made that the preferred bidder for supplying the new trams was the Spanish firm CAF (Construcciones y Auxiliar de Ferrocarriles) and the preferred tramcars were the Urbos 3 design. The aim was to have the new fleet in operation by late 2014 on the existing route. This would be followed by the opening of the extension to New Street Station in 2015.

The chosen new tramcar fleet was the CAF Urbos 3. A proven design already running on many tramways on the Continent. The trams were also capable of mounting the steep gradient of the proposed extension along Pinfold Street.

In January 2012 the plans for the redirection of traffic in Birmingham city centre were published to fore-warn drivers of road closures and changes as part of the building and operation of the Tramway. The city centre route was to run from Snow Hill Station to New Street Station via Bull Street, Corporation Street, Stephenson Hill and Stephenson Street, with a reversing stub near the end of Stephenson Street. Bus routes and drivers of other vehicles were required to take to side streets to avoid the construction work. Final Government approval was passed in February.

At 9.30am on 16 March 2012 there was another incident involving a car and the Tramway, though this time no tram was involved. A Mercedes car, driven by a 44-year old male, somehow entered the reserved track and demolished fencing at The Royal tram stop. The car was irreparably damaged, though the driver was unhurt. He said, "I was turning the corner when I lost control, went across the tracks and smashed into the barrier". Tram services in the area were disrupted for around an hour with services terminating at The Crescent, Bilston.

Posters appeared in Birmingham city centre advertising the building of the Metro extension. Note that the picture shows a T69 tramcar in Broad Street, when they were not capable of climbing up the Pinfold Street gradient and it also shows overhead wires, when this section of track was to be overhead free.

Work on the Westside extension began. Construction was deliberately scheduled to take many years and carried out in short phases. This was to reduce the impact to the public and traders with shops in the area. The first phase was to extend the Tramway from just before Snow Hill Station to run along the outside of the station on a new bridge, then along to terminate in Bull Street. The next phase was an extension from Bull Street along Corporation Street, Stephenson Place into Stephenson Street to terminate outside New Street Station. This stop was to be named "Grand Central" (the name of the shopping centre above New Street Station). The proposal included turning Corporation Street into a pedestrian and tram only thoroughfare, which required redirecting bus routes that had a peak period usage of 140 buses an hour. The extension was anticipated to cost £128 million. On 13 June 2012 Norman Baker, Minister of Transport, symbolically dug a sod of earth at the junction of Corporation and Bull Streets to mark the start of building the extension to New Street Railway Station. In fact, the main works did not start until the following year 2013.

As previously noted, the Metro bridge over Great Bridge Road had been the scene of many crashes where lorries that were too high attempted (unsuccessfully) to drive under the bridge. Since 2006 more than twenty lorries had hit the bridge, despite it being fitted with large warning signs and lights that flash if an over-height vehicle approached it. June 2012 was no exception, when yet another lorry became wedged under the bridge.

Cars numbers 05 and 10 at Wednesbury Parkway with car 05 on its way to Wolverhampton, while car 10 is on the siding leading to the depot..

The publicity department of the Metro had a great idea in September 2012. The Tramway had achieved a 99% reliability record during the year and to spread the message the public relations department went to Snow Hill Station with an ice cream van to give away "99" ice creams in celebration of the landmark achievement. It was a hot day and free ice cream was an offer most travellers could not refuse and in around two hours over 600 ice creams had been given away. Councillor Kath Hartley, Vice Chairman of Centro, said: "The Midland Metro is a real success story in the West Midlands, due in no small part to such a high punctuality record, so I am delighted we have been able to celebrate that with the public." There was no mention that the initial specification of the Tramway was for a six-minute service all day, while the actual service fell far short of this.

The developer Argenta offered £25 million to the Council to help fund the extension of the Metro from New Street Station to Centenary Square. Argent are developers specialising in inner city regeneration. They promoted the developments in Brindley Place and Paradise Circus, both of which are close to the west side extension of the Tramway. Sir Albert Bore, Birmingham Labour Party Leader and at this time Leader of the Council said "Argent's track record for successfully delivering big city centre regeneration projects not just in Birmingham with Brindley Place but across the UK, sets the tone for the high quality development the city deserves."

In the latter half of 2012 the Government announced that they were changing the way major transport proposals were to be funded. Instead of funding individual projects they would distribute funding according to population and priorities decided by new Local Transport Bodies. However, there was no indication of the total amount of funding that would be distributed.

Changes were needed to prepare for the arrival of the new tramcar fleet as all the platforms at the tram stops needed modifications. The Urbos 3 trams were 17cm (six inches) wider than the T69 trams. This necessitated the closure of the whole system from Easter Sunday, 30 March, to 15 April 2013 while the platforms were narrowed to make room to accommodate the new trams. During the shutdown passengers were able to use Metro and Metro/Bus tickets and passes on bus services along the route. The T69 tram doorways were fitted with short floor extensions to prevent passengers from trapping their feet between the tram and the edge of the platform.

In the middle of 2013, the Tramway was informed that the first of the 21 new CAF trams was ready to be shipped to England. The new tramcars had a passenger carrying capacity of 210 people, including 54 seated (the existing T69 trams had a capacity for 156 passengers). Unfortunately, the good news was tempered by more problems with the overhead wiring at Soho Benson Road, leading to service cancella-tions in June.

On 22 November 2013 there was an example of a rare accident caused by a tramcar. At 9.45am on the Bilston Road, Priestfield a tramcar collided with a van queueing in traffic. The van was pushed forward causing damage to three vehicles in front of it (two lorries and a car). The collision occurred at low speed and nobody was injured as a result. A police spokesman said, "Officers are currently trying to establish the full circumstances which led to the collision and are appealing for anyone who witnessed the incident to come forward." It was necessary to terminate the tramway service at Priestfield for several hours while the vehicles were removed.

A passenger survey of passengers using West Midlands public transport found that there was more satisfaction by users of the Metro (90%) than those using buses (79%). Also, passengers considered that the Metro gave better value for money (63%) than buses (50%) and trains (61%).

The first of the new CAF tramcars arrived from Spain in early October. To mark the delivery a small ceremony took place when Sir Albert Bore, Birmingham City Council Leader, officially unveiled the tramcar that was numbered 17, the next fleet number after the last of the old fleet. The new tramway stop to be built outside New Street Station was named "Grand Central" after the rebuilt shopping centre in the station. The existing stop in Snow Hill Station was moved to the north end of the station and renamed "St Chad's". The next stage of the expansion, to Centenary Square was approved by the City Council at a cost of £42.4 million.

The first of the Urbos 3 tramcars from CAF was unveiled to the press in October 2013. Here it is in the newly extended depot at Wednesbury with Birmingham City Council leader Sir Albert Bore aboard. Photo Midland Metro.

The development of the new HS2 railway line from London raised speculation that it could mean a new line for the Metro to link New Street Station with the new HS2 station and possibly be extended to the NEC and the airport. However to add to the confusion, the City Council raised the idea of a monorail (again) to run from New Street station to the airport. For the extension of the Tramway to the HS2 station two possible routes were identified. One from Bull Street/Corporation Street, to Lower Bull Street, right into High Street, Carrs Lane, Moor Street Queensway, to Curzon Street the other from Bull Street/Corporation Street, to Lower Bull Street, crossing Dale End, to New Meeting Street, Moor Street Queensway and Curzon Street. There was also speculation that the line could be extended to serve Coventry, though there was an alternative proposal for a bus route to connect Coventry with the airport.

At the beginning of 2014 some Councillors raised the idea that the free travel on the Metro for pensioners who were West Midlands residents should be removed and they should pay like everyone else. Within a few weeks the idea was dropped, when Councillors realised that pensioners were the group with the highest proportion of active voters and it was not a good idea to alienate them by removing this small benefit.

As part of the public relations initiatives one of the new trams (number 20) was put on public display outside New Street Station. The public were impressed with the tram and further displays were arranged at St Georges and Wednesbury depot. The public saw progress on the extensions when a length of track was laid along Stephenson Street. It was also announced that the extension to New Street Station was expected to raise the number of passengers per year to eight million from five million.

The Prime Minister announced on 7 June that there would be a £350 million investment for the West Midlands including Metro extensions to Edgbaston, Curzon Street (for the HST2 station) and Broad Street. On 5 September the first four new CAF trams entered public service and, by the end of August, 12 new trams had arrived from Spain.

There was a rather unusual event on the Tramway during the summer. For just one week tram number 12 ran with an unofficial nameplate. The name "Ernie" appeared on one side of one end of the tram. The nameplate came from the depot battery shunter, though who Ernie was is a mystery. It appeared that the management were unaware of the move of the nameplate for a week. Once the jape became known to officialdom, the nameplate was returned to the depot shunter.

Tram number 12 carried an unofficial nameplate for about a week in the summer of 2014. It is believed that it only carried one nameplate.

In September 2014, an unexpected but not unusual problem was discovered when the track between Priestfield and St George's was having a planned replacement. When the old track-bed was removed, a Victorian mine shaft was discovered near The Royal stop. It had been capped with a concrete cover some years ago, but the recent works had disturbed it. The contractors carried out an investigation prior to filling in the shaft. The additional work delayed the re-opening of the line to St Georges well beyond the planned twelve weeks closure.

A welcome boost to the confidence of Midland Metro came in 2014 when the Tramway won three prestigious awards at the global Light Rail Awards in London. National Express West Midlands (operator of the Metro) won Operator of the Year. CAF, manufacturers of the Metro's Urbo 3 tramcars won supplier of the year and Project of the Year was won by Centro for the introduction of the new trams into service.

However, the end of 2014 ended badly for the Metro. The second half of December saw a significant number of interruptions to the tramway, with the tram service being disrupted for thirteen of the last eighteen working days. A spokesman for Midland Metro operator National Express said: "We are sorry for the inconvenience caused to our customers during the recent disruption. The Midland Metro is currently undergoing its largest ever engineering project. This major work has been further complicated by the discovery of a mine shaft at The Royal. We are working hard with our partners Centro and local Councils to ensure that any disruption is minimised, and services return to normal as soon as possible." To add to passengers woes there were above inflation fare increases on the Metro that took effect on Friday 2 January 2015.

Tramcar number 35 "Angus Adams" in the first CAF livery. Note the self adhesive nameplate.

The purchase of the new CAF trams meant that the depot required extending. The new building was opened on 5 February 2015 by Councillor Darren Cooper, the leader of Sandwell Borough Council and a member of the West Midlands Integrated Transport Authority. Tramcar number 23 was driven through a large banner declaring "Midland Metro Depot Extension Open 5 February 2015". The start of a new era for the Tramway was emphasised when the last of the T69 tramcars (number 16) was withdrawn from service on 14 August 2015. The service was now run entirely by the new CAF trams. 17 were in service while numbers 17, 34, 36 and 37 were yet to enter service.

As the Tramway developed it was found that the second platform at Wolverhampton, St Georges, had become redundant. It was used in 2014 to display to the public tram number 20, one of the new CAF Urbos 3 tramcars. The following year, 2015, the northern track was removed and it was used as a coach drop off point. However, it was little used by the public and the stop was used by Banga Bus for a while, but now seems redundant. Trams continue to use the southern platform. When the Wolverhampton Station exten-sion opens it is proposed that the main service will be to the terminus at the railway station, while a limited service goes to St Georges.

A major landmark was achieved on 24 October 2015 when the Snow Hill platform stop was closed. The service temporarily terminated at St Pauls while the connection was made to link the new tracks of the ex-tension with the existing tracks from St Pauls. A new tram stop to replace the Snow Hill stop was still be-ing built, so a temporary stop was built alongside the railway station. It was unusual as there was limited space and the platforms were staggered. This was closed when the new St Chads stop was opened on 2 June 2016. The new section to Bull Street was used on 19 November when the Queen named tram num-ber 35 "Angus Adams" after the former Chairman of Centro and a prime mover for the extension of the tramway from Snow Hill to New Street, who had died suddenly in 2012 at the age of 67. As erection of the overhead wires had not yet been completed, the tram was towed to the Bull Street stop by the depot maintenance lorry. Services to the stop opened on 6 December 2015, but closed after a short time until 2016 due to an 8 week pause due to Christmas shopping. There was a change in the way the name of the tram was applied. Instead of brass nameplates being bolted to the tramcar, the name was printed on self adhesive plastic that was stuck near the front of the tramcar.

The tramway finished 2015 in an optimistic mood, with a brand new fleet of trams and its first extension being built the future looked positive.

The named T69 tramcars had cast metal nameplates. This is tramcar number 10, named "John Stanley Webb", the tramway historian. The named CAF trams were given trans-fer names.

Tramcars numbers 23 and 35 on the hill of Pinfold Street. Next stop for number 23 is New Street Station while number 35 is climbing the hill to terminate at the Library.

CHAPTER 7

A New Fleet and Expansion of the system 2016 - 2019

It was announced that the new extension of track from New Street Station (Grand Central) to Centenary Square (the Library) would be catenary free and that the trams would be fitted with batteries in order to work that section. This was a retrofit as when the trams were purchased the batteries then available were not powerful enough for the trams to drive up the gradient of Pinfold Street. Since then battery technology improved and the trams could be fitted with more powerful batteries. The programme was funded by Greater Birmingham and Solihull Local Enterprise Partnership (£3.15 million) and UK Tram (£1 million). It was also planned that the extension from Centenary Square to Five Ways would also be catenary-free. Then from Five Ways along Broad Street to Edgbaston overhead working would be resumed. The proposed Eastside extension would also be catenary-free between the HS2 station and Digbeth High Street in order to allow trams to pass under a low railway bridge. In Wolverhampton the extension to Piper's Row and the Station would also be without overhead catenary. It was estimated that the savings on overhead costs while building the extension would be £650,000.

Meanwhile construction of the line in the city centre continued with the section from Bull Street stop to New Street Station (the stop being named Grand Central after the nearby shopping centre) via Corporation Street (where there was another stop) and Stephenson Street. Car 37 ran testing trials at night in early May 2016. Services were scheduled to start running from Bull Street to New Street Station from Sunday 22 May but were delayed by track alignment works due to the rails not being level at the bend in Stephenson Street. Centro's Midland Metro programme director Phil Hewitt said: *"It is bitterly disappointing as everything else is in place and ready to go but, as we have said right from the start, safety is paramount."* The new line was opened to tram services on 30 May 2016.

Tramcars numbers 25 and 28 at the Wednesbury Great Western Street stop during short working due to removal of the Arthur Street road bridge in Bilston.

In the morning of 29 May 2016 trams from Wolverhampton were forced to terminate early due to a car blocking the tracks in Birmingham City centre, causing chaos for passengers. Hundreds were forced to walk to the city centre for the weekend festival. The car was left straddling the tracks next to Snow Hill Station, meaning trams were unable to reach the Bull Street stop for more than three hours. After announcing the blockage at 8am, Midland Metro explained why the trams were disrupted and that passengers had to take a bus, train or walk from St Paul's.

Tramcar number 37 was named "Ozzy Osborne", after the member of Birmingham band Black Sabbath, who unveiled it on 26 May 2016 at the inauguration of the new extension. He rode the tram from Navigation Street to New Street Station. Not everyone congratulated the Tramway on the extension. Some critics pointed out that the rate of track laying was a meagre 81cm (32 inches) a day meaning the extension took four years to complete. However, there was some good news, the Department of Transport gave approval for the extension from New Street Station to Centenary Square.

Tramcar number 37 was named "Ozzy Osborne" after the member of the rock group "Black Sabbeth". Ozzy Osbourne performed the naming at the new tram stop in Corporation Street accompanied by Cllr John Clancy, leader of Birmingham City Council, and Cllr Roger Lawrence, Chairman of the ITA.

When tram 37 was repainted in the blue livery the name was reapplied, however, with a matching blue background to match the new colours of the vehicle.

Initially a temporary stop was introduced at the side entrance to Snow Hill Station to replace the closed stop inside the station. However, there was insufficient space for a substantive stop and a new stop was built at the north end of Snow Hill Station platforms. Called Snow Hill, this was opened on 2 June 2016 and the temporary arrangements near the front entrance of the station ceased. However, access between the new stop and the station entrance was difficult. So the stop was renamed St Chads in January 2017, after the nearby Roman Catholic Cathedral. Passengers for the railway station were advised to alight at Bull Street as the walk from there to the railway station was all level.

Cars 24 (right) and 26 at the St Chads tram stop at the end of Snow Hill Station. The single disused track to the left is the abandoned tram track into Snow Hill Stop.

Car 25 halts at a deserted St Chads stop one Tuesday morning. Exits are either at the far end of the platform to descend stairs or to walk past the photographer along the side of the track to access Colmore Row and the front of the railway station.

Up to 16 June 2016 the trams, buses and trains were co-ordinated by the West Midlands Passenger Transport Executive under the operating name Centro. It was responsible for implenting policies set by the West Midlands Integrated Transport Authority. In June 2016 a new body, Transport for West Midlands (TfWM), was established that took over the functions, responsibilities, assets and staff of both of the organisations. The brand name "Network West Midlands" was kept to minimise confusion for the public.

The 19 June 2016 saw a major disruption to passengers on the tramway from 5.30pm. The overhead line broke between Black Lake and West Bromwich Central and passengers had to walk along the track to ride on shuttle trams either side of the damage. Repairs to the damage were not completed until 21 June. This unfortunately coincided with problems on the London Midland Trains between Stafford and Wolverhampton due to signalling issues. Passengers travelling from Wolverhampton to Birmingham via tram had to take a normal tram from Wolverhampton St George's to Black Lake, walk from Black Lake to Dudley Street, board a shuttle service from Dudley Street to West Bromwich Central and then board a normal service car from West Bromwich Central to Grand Central, Birmingham. Passengers heading from Birmingham to Wolverhampton faced the same complicated journey in reverse. Then from 22.00 on Wednesday, trams from Wolverhampton terminated at Black Lake to allow repair work to be carried out, with no services running between Black Lake and Grand Central.

The tramway service in Birmingham centre was disrupted early in October 2016 by protesters in wheel-chairs campaigning against the government with banners with the message that "TORY CUTS KILL". They blocked the tramway where it crosses Colmore Row, by Snow Hill Station. Having made their point, they dispersed when police arrived to move them on.

As part of the preparations for catenary-free operation tramcar 18 was sent back to the CAF factory at Zaragoza for the fitting of lithium-ion batteries. The cost of fitting batteries to the whole fleet was £15.5 million, which was expected to save on infrastructure costs. On an historical note, this made the Metro the first British second-generation tramway to run in streets using battery power. A structural and environmental survey was also carried out on the track bed of the former South Staffordshire Railway between the Wednesbury Great Western Street depot and near to Brierley Hill town centre. .

Fitting the batteries for wire-free operation. The upper photograph shows the trams as delivered without batteries, but having space on the roof to have them fitted at a later date. The lower photo shows a tramcar with roof-mounted batteries fitted and ready for the sections of the route without overhead wires.

2016 was a good year for awards for the Metro. At the Global Light Rail Awards in November 2016 the Metro won Project of the Year Over €50 million (for the city centre extension) and Best Customer Initiative (for the introduction of contactless payments). Then later in the month the joint delivery team of Transport for West Midlands (TfWM) and Balfour Beatty won the Construction Project of the Year.

Plans were made for rebuilding Wolverhampton Station. These include the provision of a new terminus stop for the Metro extension serving the station. At the other end of the line the new stop that had opened on 1 January 2017 at the north end of Snow Hill Station was given the name "St Chads". The stop provided access to local businesses, including the new office blocks One and Two Snow Hill. There was a disadvantage as passengers wanting to catch a train at Snow Hill had to descend to the street level and walk a short distance to a new side entrance to the station in Livery Street via Lionel Street.

Plans were made for the rebuilding of Wolverhampton Station. These include the provision of a new terminus stop for the Midland Metro extension to serve the station. At the other end of the line the new stop that had opened on 1 January 2017 at the north end of Snow Hill Station was given the name "St Chads". The stop provided access to local businesses, including the new office blocks One and Two Snow Hill. There was a disadvantage as passengers wanting to catch a train at Snow Hill had to descend to the street level and walk some distance to the main entrance to the station. Passengers wanting an easier access to the station from the tram stop were able to do so after work was completed to allow access to the station's second entrance in Livery Street via Lionel Street.

At 6.00am on the morning of 31 January 2017 the new extension to the tramway became blocked when a lorry drove onto the reserved track alongside Snow Hill Station. As this section of track had been grassed the lorry got bogged down, blocking both tracks. The driver had been heading for the M6 but took the wrong turning alongside the railway station and ended up on the tram track. Removing the lorry from the track took five hours, during which trams terminated at the St Paul's stop. A Midland Metro spokesman said "Due to a lorry blocking the line at St Chad's, we were only operating from Wolverhampton to St Paul's only. It also meant one or two trams were stranded on the section between Grand Central and Snow Hill." Trams continued to turn short at St Paul's while the track was inspected for damage.

The Tramway announced that the extension in Birmingham city centre had brought around 300,000 extra new customers in November and December. The route into Birmingham Snow Hill lies alongside the railway track in tunnels and a cutting. This made it relatively invisible to the public (potential customers). The city centre extension along Bull Street, Corporation Street and Navigation Street took the tramway into the heart of the area most used by Birmingham's commuters and shoppers. The public responded by making far more use of the system. The number of passengers carried on the line was 4.8 million in 2017, then in 2018 it rose to 6.2 million, and in 2019 it was 5.7 million.

A 19-year-old man died after being hit by a tram on the reserved track near Kenrick Park. The police appealed for information following the incident on 6 June 2017 after they were called to the tram stop near Devereux Road at 7.40pm. The death was treated as unexplained. Officers were working to establish the circumstances of how he came to be on the tracks.

Despite the no entry sign, the ending of a road surface, replaced by grass, and a ditch at the end of the road surface, a lorry managed to drive onto it and got bogged down as the mud tracks show. Snow Hill railway station lies immediately behind the wall on the left.

Work on the Wolverhampton extension started in mid-June to replace track in Bilston Road and at St George's including the installation of points to take the Tramway along Pipers Row and Railway Drive to the station. It was expected that the new track would be open by Christmas 2020. The Tramway announced that the expansion programme would include 700m of new track from Bilston Street to Wolverhampton Railway Station; New Street Station to Centenary Square and Paradise Circus 840m; Centenary Square to Edgbaston 1.35km; the Eastside extension to Digbeth 1.7km; Brierley Hill 11km: East Birmingham to Solihull, NEC and airport 16km (opening 2026). This gave a total network of 31.5km, an increase of 14km. Birmingham's new Mayor said that he expected the extension to Five Ways to be fully open in 2020.

Car 10 turns to run alongside Snow Hill station on its way to Wolverhampton. Despite the no entry signs various vehicles have attempted to drive along the tram route, to run into trouble when they run out of hard surface and sink into grass and mud.

Looking up Bull Street from Corporation Street. The road signage is very clear, any vehicles except trams are prohibited from entering Corporation Street and must turn left, away from the tram route.

Tramcar number 20 is just leaving Priestfield stop and heads towards Wolverhampton. It only travelled as far as the points where it reversed, crossing to the other track in order to return to Birmingham. The short working was caused by major road works in 2019 necessitated by installing points in the existing trackwork for the extension to the railway station.

The work in Wolverhampton was to take six months during which the tram service would terminate at Priestfield. The impact of this work on passenger numbers was greater than had been expected, particularly at weekends. Passenger numbers over the whole network fell 18% on Saturdays and 20% on Sundays. Compared with the previous year the overall numbers were down by around 10%. Following the re-opening of the line to St George's there was some recovery of passenger numbers.

In mid-June, the business plan for the Brierley Hill extension was sent to the Secretary of State for Transport. The line from Bull Street to the airport continued to be developed at a cost of £735 million. It is expected to take nine years to build. The 2018 Transport Plan included proposals for a route from Wolverhampton to Wednesfield and New Cross Hospital. In September, the Department of Transport agreed to fund £59.8 million, bringing the total funding to the £149 million required for the project. The opening was anticipated to be 2021.

There was an unusual incident at the Wednesbury Parkway stop in Leabrook North Road in the afternoon of 16 August 2017. This stop has a car park and a small fire started in a hedge beside the parking area. It soon spread to one of the parked cars and the Fire Brigade was called. Before the Brigade arrived, the fire had spread, and six cars were soon ablaze. The fire was quickly extinguished, but all six cars were severely damaged.

There was another death on the line when a tram hit a man near the Jewellery Quarter stop on 30 September 2017. Police cordoned off roads in the area and the tram service was curtailed. The death was treated as being unexplained.

On 20 November 2017 the Government announced that £250 million had been allocated to the Metro for "better transport" that will be used to fund the new route from Wednesbury to Brierley Hill, via Dudley Town centre. Birmingham was chosen as the host city for the 2022 Commonwealth Games. As part of the preparations for the games, the West Midlands Combined Authority committed £50 million to support the tram Interchange at Wolverhampton station. To be ready for the games the Edgbaston extension was to be brought forward by a year. The withdrawn fleet of T69 trams had all been moved to Long Marston for storage. Hopes that they could be sold for further service on another tramway proved fruitless and they were sold for scrap in an "as seen" condition, as some had been cannibalised to provide spares for other tramcars.

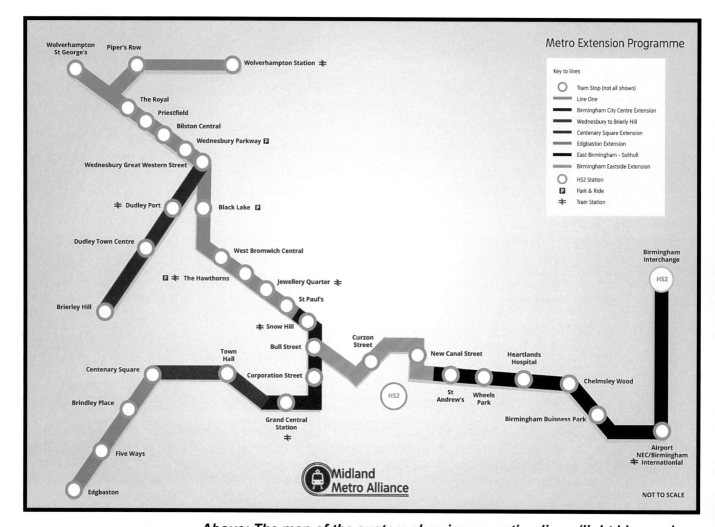

Above: The map of the system showing operating lines (light blue and purple) and proposed lines in various stages of building. The extension of the network had taken far longer than had been hoped. By the end of 2017 the system was actively progressing to Wolverhampton Station and Centenary Square with preparatory work progressing to Edgbaston. The other routes were in the early stages of moving utilities and preparation.

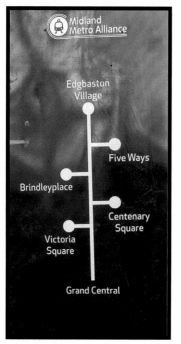

Left: Along the site of engineering works the tramway placed posters detailing the proposed new lines.

Tram number 18 arrived back from Spain in late 2017 with its new roof-mounted batteries. It commenced trials while waiting for the Secretary if State to approve it for carrying passengers. It was able to carry its first passengers in March and part of the testing included running part of the route with the pantograph down (despite there being an overhead) to test the wire-free operation. The work to change the remainder of the CAF fleet was undertaken in-house, starting with tramcar number 31 and all trams were converted by the end of 2019. Tram 26 had been damaged in a depot accident in June 2017 and was sent to Wolverton railway workshops for repairs. It returned in March 2018, apparently ready to go back into service. However, it remained in the depot until June 2019, when it finally returned to service.

Tramcar number 36 at the temporary terminus at the Library stop. The pantograph is down as there is no overhead wire from Grand Central stop, the trams run on their batteries. The decorated building in the background is the new Central Library.

The year 2018 did not have a good start for the Metro extension. The development relied on a number of other projects to enable the new line to Five Ways to be built. Unfortunately, the major construction firm Carillion went into liquidation in January. The Company had many projects in the Midlands including the £500 million rebuilding of Paradise Circus. A spokesman for the Midland Metro Alliance said work had not been affected to date but "the demolition of the former Birmingham Conservatoire as part of the Paradise development is key to extending the tram to Centenary Square and delays may impact on our pro-gramme".

Early in 2018 the Tramway announced that they would be bringing forward the purchase of 50 more tram-cars to meet the needs of the new routes and expansions of existing ones. The expansion to Five Ways would require an extra 7 to 9 vehicles in 2021. 22 would be needed in 2022 for the Brierley Hill route and a further 20 in 2026 for the Eastside route. One of the T69 trams, number 11 "Theresa Stewart", was select-ed to be preserved in a museum or heritage tramway (it is unlikely to be the Black Country Museum as the tram is the wrong gauge for that line). Disappointingly there was a drop in the annual ridership of 1% from 653,035 to 597,326. This was thought to be due to the seven-month closure of the route from Bilston Road to St George's and "driver availability issues" at the end of 2017. The situation was remedied with the training of six new drivers.

The Library became the temporary terminus of the tramway when the most recent extension was opened in December 2019. This is the view from the Library entrance looking out over the ornamental pool to the tram stop. The scene is being used for a photoshoot presumably to advertise bridal gowns as there was no sign of a bridegroom. The tram is number 27.

The low Metro bridge at Great Bridge Road, Moxley, claimed another victim when a skip lorry hit it. The accident happened about 10.00am on 26 February 2018. The police closed the road between Glyn Avenue and Constantine Way while the lorry was removed. After inspection by a structural engineer Metro trams were allowed to pass over the bridge, but at a reduced speed.

On 2 June 2018, after a report at 5.00am, the service was temporarily suspended when a body was found by police who were investigating reports of a person on the tracks at West Bromwich. Police and para-medics attended, and the person was pronounced dead at the scene

In 2018 the contract that National Express held to operate the tramways came to an end. Transport for West Midlands (the transport arm of West Midlands Combined Authority) offered a new fifteen year opera-tion and maintenance contract for the day-to-day running of the Metro. They announced that the winning bid was from Midland Metro Ltd, a not-for-profit company owned by West Midlands Combined Authority. The Transport for West Midlands Managing Director said that the series of extensions would triple the size of the system. Passenger numbers were to increase from 6.5 million to 30 million. There was a planned expansion of 1km currently being built from New Street Station to Centenary Square. Future applications would include an extension from Centenary Square to Edgbaston. Applications had already been submit-ted for extensions from Bull Street to High Street, Deritend serving Digbeth Coach Station and the Custard Factory and an extension at Wolverhampton to the Railway Station.

Metro had to pay for transport to and storage at Long Marston of the T69 trams since 2015. The cost of moving each tram was reported as £2,000 while the total storage cost was given as "approximately" £35,500 per annum. In 2017 an advertisement was placed in an e-auction. Cllr Roger Lawrence, the WMCA's lead member for transport, said: *"They've got more than a few thousand miles on the clock but in their time the T69 trams were excellent servants for the Midland Metro. They are mostly still serviceable so the auction is a good chance for someone to get themselves a bargain."* The auction was only available to registered companies and it took place on Monday January 29, 2018. However, there were no bidders. Unable to sell the redundant fleet, the decision was taken to sell thirteen of the T69 tramcars to a scrap merchant for a total of £12,000. Neither Centro nor the leaseholder of the fleet, a subsidiary of the Royal Bank of Scotland, have made public how much it cost the Metro to terminate the lease. Speculation by the press ranged from less than the £12,000 price obtained, to all the price obtained plus some more. Detailed information was not available due to "commercial confidentiality" Two tramcars were not sent for scrap. Car number 7 went to UK Trams as a rolling testbed, while number 11 was given to Birmingham Museum.

The estimated cost of the line to Solihull rose by £60 million to £735 million. On a happier note Piper's Row in Wolverhampton reopened on 2 September 2018, though the new tramway extension to the station will not open until after 2020. Also, in early September work commenced in Birmingham to extend the line from New Street Station (Grand Central) to Centenary Square (the Library). This involved closing Pinfold Street, part of New Street, Paradise Street and Centenary Square. Diversions for all traffic were set up around the back of the Crescent Theatre and the Library. Temporarily trams reversed at New Street Station leaving the headshunt free for work on the extension. The plan was to run the section of track from New Street Station to Five Ways using batteries with the overhead wiring ending at the junction of Stephenson Street and Pinfold Street.

There was another unfortunate fatality on the tramway early Saturday morning on 2 June 2018. A tramcar by Trinity Road stop struck a pedestrian just before 04.55. An ambulance was called but the staff were unable to save the individual who was pronounced dead at the scene. British Transport Police Officers were called to the stop and were working to locate the person's next of kin. For several hours the tram service only operated between Wolverhampton and West Bromwich Central. Passengers with tickets were able to use them on National Express buses and West Midlands trains.

On 24 June 2018 the operation of the Metro was transferred from Altram (a National Express subsidiary) to the West Midlands Combined Authority. The Combined Authority established a Company called Midland Metro Limited (a not for profit organisation) and the tramway was renamed West Midlands Metro. A new logo was unveiled. It was announced that they intended expanding the system and expected ridership to rise from 8 million to 30 million, turnover to rise from £12 million to £50 million and staff numbers to double from 200 to 400. These future plans were described as "an ambitious game-changing programme". Track-laying began in Wolverhampton to extend the terminus along St Georges Parade to Railway Drive. Unfortunately, the start of West Midlands Metro under new operators was not auspicious as there were over-head wiring problems that interrupted the services as it could only run on a single line between the Jewellery Quarter and Grand Central. On a more positive note two tramcars, numbers 31 and 36, were fitted with roof mounted batteries in Wednesbury Depot.

The end of Stephenson Street and the end of the overhead. The route continues behind the photographer but the trams have to run on their batteries, that are recharged when the tram car returns to overhead power. Birmingham had battery (then called accumulator) trams from 1890 to 1901, but they were found to be uneconomic to run and were replaced with more conventional electric trams.

In order to demonstrate to the public that a new operator was managing the Tramway, a new livery was introduced. It was all blue with a silver framing for the cabs. It was first seen on tramcar 30 on 16 July 2018. The West Midlands Combined Authority invited tenders to supply more new trams for the Tramway at an estimated price of £180 million. Potential suppliers were required to express an interest by 14th September detailing their manufacturing and maintenance experience, including catenary-free experience.

There was another accident on 13 August 2018 when there was a collision between a tram and a car on the Wolverhampton Ring Road. A woman in the car was taken to hospital with injuries.

The projected cost of the Brierley Hill route rose by £33 million to £343 million (due to increased cost of purchasing the land). A study looking at the viability of extending the Metro to Walsall came to the conclusion that there was not enough support locally for the initiative. A study to look at the potential for a more limited extension of the Metro from Wolverhampton to Willenhall via New Cross Hospital completed in 2018, concluded that there is insufficient demand at this time in the corridor to generate a positive business case for a Metro extension, especially if the heavy rail passenger service resumes as planned with the intermediate stations and a timetable that includes both local shuttle services and direct connections to Birmingham New Street. Consequently, with the support of West Midlands Combined Authority, Transport for West Midlands and West Midlands Trains, officers were actively progressing the new station proposals for Willenhall and Darlaston (James Bridge) as part of the 'West Midlands HS2 Connectivity Package'.

At New Street Station tram passengers had to walk back up Stephenson Street to New Street in order to access the ramp climbing to the station entrance. To make it more inviting for tram passengers a new entrance was built on the corner of the station at street level so the intending railway passengers could exit the tram and walk directly into the station, with no climb and being under shelter most of the way. The new entrance opened later in the year.

On 18 January 2019 tramcar number 33 was given the name Cyril Regis in honour of the former West Bromwich Albion player who died from a heart attack on 14 January 2018 at the age of 59. He was described as one of the England game's breakthrough black players.

Number 35 at the Library temporary terminus displays the new livery. Given the size of the concrete blocks laid across the tracks the "Stop" sign seems a little superfluous.

Looking down Broad Street towards Five Ways during the construction of the tram track. It is along this section that the tramway goes over the canal by the Gas Street Basin.

In March 2019 funding was agreed by the West Midlands Combined Authority for the expansion of the system with a route from Wednesbury to Brierley Hill via Dudley. The 11 kilometre line was expected to reach Dudley by 2023. The route would leave the Wednesbury Great Western stop and travel south west to Tipton and Dudley. Initially the cost of the extension was estimated at £343 million. This rose in 2017 to £402 million and in 2019 increased again to £449 million. The proposal included 17 stops along the route. These are Golds Hill (provisional stop); Great Bridge; Horseley Road; Dudley Port (for interchange with national rail services); Sedgley Road; Birmingham New Road; Tipton Road; Station Road (for Castle Hill attractions); Dudley town centre (at Dudley bus station); Flood Street (provisional stop); New Road (provisional stop); Cinder Bank; Pedmore Road; Canal Street (provisional stop); Waterfront; Merry Hill Centre; and Brierley Hill.

Broad Street looking the other way towards the city centre. The temporary tramway terminus at the library is immediately beyond the far fence.

On Tuesday 5 March 2019 passengers hoping to use the tramway in the centre of Birmingham found that there was a bus replacement service as the overhead wires had been damaged. Repairs took until Wednesday evening. March also saw the completion of strengthening works to the Broad Street bridge over the canal. Both the road and the canal were closed to allow the work to be carried out. Starting in December 2018 the work involved installing strengthening steelwork under the bridge. Scheduled to take twelve weeks, it was completed two days early, enabling canal traffic to pass under the strengthened bridge. Broad Street itself remained closed for tracklaying.

There was another incident in the middle of April 2019 when a member of the public collapsed while crossing Corporation Street. This blocked the tram tracks causing the trams to have to turn short at Bull Street. An ambulance was called to attend to the man and the tram service was disrupted for some time.

The Midland Metro had opened on 30 May 1999, so it celebrated its 20th Anniversary in 2019. To mark the occasion tramcar number 19 was repainted in a special commemorative livery of mainly white with some silver and blue. Appropriately, it was first shown to the public on 30 May 2019. Later cars numbers 21 and 36 were given a similar livery but carrying all over advertisements. The Metro announced that the tram service travelled more than 2 million kilometres per year, carrying more than seven million passengers.

In May 2019 tramcar number 19 was painted in a special livery to commemorate the 20th anniversary of the opening of the Tramway. Here it is seen turning from Stephenson Place into Stephenson Street alongside New Street Station.

The construction of the tramway from the Library to Five Ways, along Broad Street began in Spring 2019. The work involved the entire closing of that section of Broad Street for at least two years. The proposal is that the Five Ways underpass will to be restricted to trams only, all other road traffic would have to use the raised roundabout. The purchasing process for more new trams for the extensions was proceeding. Bids had been received from Alstom, Bombardier, CAF and Skoda. On 7 October 2019 the Tramway selected CAF as the supplier. The contract was to supply 21 Urbos trams with catenary-free capability at a cost of £83.5M, with an option for 29 further trams. The contract included technical support, battery management and spares for 30 years. West Midlands Metro chose CAF to supply an additional 21 Urbos trams with catenary-free capability at a cost of £83.5M. The contract was announced on the 7 October, with an option for 29 more trams which CAF will also provide. Just one T69 tram remained at Wednesbury Depot, number 16 as it had been kept as a potential works tramcar. However, in August it too was transferred to Long Marston to join 07, 10 and 11. Trams 07 and 10 were transferred to UKTram, while tram 11 was donated to Birmingham Museum for display.

In June 2019 a public bench celebrating the Birmingham rock group "Black Sabbath" was erected on the Broad Street bridge over the canal. Images of the members of the band, Geezer Butler, Tony Iommi, Ozzy Osbourne and Bill Ward form part of the installation. Members of the public resting on the bench will be able to watch tramcars going to and fro between Birmingham city centre and the Edgbaston terminus. The bench was unveiled by Geezer Butler and Tony Iommi. It was the idea of "super-fan" and architect Mohammed Osam and the installation includes renaming the location Black Sabbath Bridge.

The tribute to the original members of Black Sabbath, the Birmingham heavy rock group.

In August 2019 the BBC revealed that the £137 million east side extension would be delayed due to uncertainties about the building of the HS2 station at Curzon Street. The extension was planned to reach Digbeth, passing under the Curzon Street HS2 station. However, uncertainties have delayed the Government's final decision regarding the railway station. This has put back the expected opening of the tramway to 2026. Though the new tram route was seen by HS2 as a vital part of the development of Curzon Street Station. It had been planned to open the station in time for the Commonwealth, however, the delays meant that the deadline to have the scheme open in time for the Commonwealth Games had now been missed and instead the line will be built in two halves and connected in the middle once HS2 has built its station. Laura Shoaf, managing director of TfWM, said "the original plan was to have the extension completed by 2022. We've been unable to achieve that in part because of the delay in the build of [Curzon Street] station itself. What we're trying now to do is to achieve the best result we can."

30 August 2019 was a historic day for modern tramways in Britain. Late in the evening tram number 28 did the first test run up Pinfold Street to Paradise Street on the catenary-free section of the Tramway. This was the first time a modern British tramcar ran in the street using just battery power. Another red-letter day happened during the night of 24 October when tram number 28 became the first tram to run on its batteries all the way to the Library at Centenary Square. The change from overhead power to batteries was quick and most of the passengers would be entirely unaware of the change of power source. Indeed the only sign that batteries were being used was seeing the trams move with their pantographs lowered.

There was a small hiccup in the new livery in October 2019. Tram number 37, which had been given the full blue livery had to have a replacement panel. The only one available was in the old magenta colour. It was fitted and the tram ran for a short while sporting a magenta corner panel. It was re-vinyled with the correct blue colour as soon as possible.

The Wolverhampton section of the line, where The Tramway shares the road with other traffic, continued to be problematic. In the eight months between the middle of March and the beginning of December there were seven collisions between cars and trams on the road running section. The first happened at 4.00pm on Sunday 17 March when a car collided with a tram at the car park at Priestfield stop on the Metro. The car was pushed about 3m down the tram track. The car driver was taken to hospital as a precaution and the tramway was able to resume its full service at 5.30pm. On Wednesday 24 April a van collided with a tram. Once again Priestfield became the temporary terminus for Wolverhampton trams. The A41 Bilston Road curse struck again on Tuesday 21 May when a car crossing the tramway track stalled directly in front of moving tramcar number 18 and again at 3.00pm on Friday 21 June after a lorry crashed into a tram, again in Bilston Road. The Royal and St Georges tram stops were closed for an hour while the damaged vehicles were removed. A more serious accident occurred at 8.20am on 19 August in the rush hour when tram number 31 (named Cyril Regis) collided with an SUV while crossing the roundabout on the ring road. The tram was de-railed and the car overturned, trapping the female driver who had to be cut from her vehi-cle by firefighters. The roundabout had to be closed to allow the fire brigade to release the car driver. The tram driver and four passengers were treated at the scene and discharged. The crash

was caused by the car driver running through a red light on the Bilston Road/Ring Road Island. It took some time to re-rail the tramcar and tow it back to the depot for repairs. These took nearly seven months and the tram did not re-turn to service until 5 March 2020. Then a fifth accident occurred at 8.30am on 3 December, again on the Bilston Road. There was a collision between a tramcar and a car. Though the tram suffered a smashed window there were no injuries to anyone. Following trams terminated at Priestfield stop while the vehicles involved in the accidents were cleared away. The full tram service resumed after an hour.

Tram number 28 was given the name "Jasper Carrott" after the Birmingham born comedian. He performed the unveiling ceremony at the Town Hall tram stop, before the extension was officially opened to the public.

On 13 November Jasper Carrott arrived by tram at the Town Hall stop and went around to the front of tram number 28 to unveil his name as the tram had been named in his honour. He was accompanied by his wife Hazel on this special trip (the line beyond Grand Central had not yet been opened to the public). By the end of November all the trams had been repainted in the new operator's livery of all blue with a silver outline for the two cabs. All the new trams were retrofitted with batteries by the end of 2019 in readiness for the public opening of the catenary-free section between Grand Central and Centenary Square.

In October 2019, following a tendering process, the Metro announced that a further 21 tramcars had been ordered from CAF in an order worth £83.5 million for delivery commencing 2021, bringing the fleet to over 70 trams. The new trams will be needed when the initial route is extended to Hagley Road, then in Wolverhampton to the Station and the major extension from Wednesbury to Brierley Hill. The new trams will be to the third generation "Urbos" design and will be fitted for battery operation over the catenary-free sections of the extended network. Following the initial stages of expansion from Grand Central (New Street Station) to Centenary Square the numbers of passengers rose from five million a year to seven million. The purchase contracts includes technical support, battery management and an option to purchase a further 29 trams as the network expands. CAF will provide long term maintenance, repair, overhaul, and renewal of the batteries for a 30 year period.

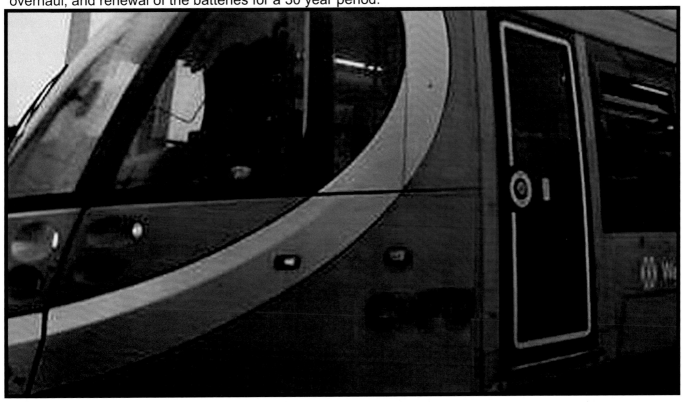

Tram number 29 was named "Cupid", one of Santa's reindeer, for the Christmas season 2019/2020.

Andy Street, the Mayor of the West Midlands, said: "These new trams are a real game-changer for our expanding West Midlands Metro network and I am delighted we have put pen to paper with CAF. These next generation trams are battery powered, designed to operate on new sections of the line between Grand Central and Hagley Road, which are free of overhead cables. Our existing fleet of CAF trams already provide excellent service for thousands of travellers a day on the current Metro line, and these are also being modified with the installation of on-board batteries."

Cllr Ian Ward, WMCA portfolio holder for transport and leader of Birmingham City Council said: "This contract represents a huge step forward in our plans to serve even more communities across the region. Our extensions in Birmingham and Wolverhampton city centres will enable more people to easily get to places they need for work and wonderful visitor attractions like the Library of Birmingham and Symphony Hall. While the extension to Brierley Hill will unlock opportunities for many people in the Black Country." Richard Garner, CAF's UK Director, commented: "CAF is delighted to have been selected to provide additional state-of-the-art Urbos trams for this ground-breaking UK Metro line. The CAF Urbos tram will be the first example of battery technology being used in a high intensity passenger service here in the UK. The Urbos modern, spacious design will provide passengers with a quiet, smooth and comfortable travel experience."

Looking as if it is in the middle of the countryside, this section of track in the city centre runs alongside Snow Hill Station. Car 25 is heading for New Street Station and then Broad Street.

Car 25 again, this time in Stephenson Street passing Piccadilly Arcade on its way to Grand Central (New Street) Station.

As part of the Scottish celebrations for Christmas, Edinburgh Tramway temporarily named some of its trams after Santa's reindeer. The Metro soon followed suit and early in November nine tramcars appeared each named after one of Santa's reindeer. These were 17 Dancer; 20 Prancer; 22 Dasher; 23 Comet; 26 Donner; 29 Cupid; 33 Vixen; 34 Blitzen and 36 Rudolf. When the T69 trams were given names the tram-way followed the railway tradition of having cast brass or bronze nameplates. Four were fixed to each tram, two at each end. When the Urbos 3 tramcars were named, the name was printed on a self-adhesive plastic sheet the background colour of the blue livery and the lettering in black. This meant that temporary names could be applied (such as the reindeer) and removed at a later date. In the case of Santa's helpers the names were removed in January 2020.

At the top of Pinfold Street , the absence of overhead wires allows an unobstructed view of the Town Hall with the tram route curving to pass across its frontage on the way to Broad Street.

Building the tram extension from New Street Station (Grand Central) to Centenary Square (the Library) required the moving of two iconic statues. That of the "Iron Man" (by Anthony Gormley) that was outside the Council House and the Boulton, Watt and Murdock group that were outside the Registry Office (now the House of Sport) and both were placed in storage. The opening to the public of the overhead-free sec-tion from New Street Station (Grand Central) to Centenary Square (the Library) was carried out with the minimum of publicity or fuss. There had been a rumour that the extension would open to the public on the 11 December, however, no tram service appeared at the start of the day. There had been a problem on Tuesday 10 December when issues with overhead wires near the Bradley Lane stop meant that there was no service between Wednesbury Parkway and Wolverhampton St George's. This disruption delayed the intended opening of the Centenary Square extension and it was not until 11.00am that tram 36 (named "Rudolf" for the Christmas season) ran the first passenger carrying tramcar along the new extension. Sub-sequent trams all ran along the extension.

The year 2019 ended optimistically with the Birmingham extension to Centenary Square recently opened and the first part of the Wolverhampton extension being built. No one was expecting that 2020 would bring an unprecedented change to everyone's life with the news of an outbreak of Coronavirus in a city in China.

The new extension starts with a double track running along the outside of Snow Hill Station. The tram has just left St Chad's stop and drives past the station wall covered with climbing plants while the tram track has been grassed over, a surprising feature in the centre of a city. Car 25 looks very smart and ready for passengers.

CHAPTER 8

Coronavirus and the Tramway 2020 - 21

On 17 January 2020, the Transport Secretary, Grant Shapps, opened a Regional Co-ordination Centre that provides a single hub for the West Midlands Transport Authorities, Emergency Services, and Bus, Rail and Tram Operators to manage the network during major events or incidents. It was the first such centre in the UK. Little did the authorities realise the major emergency that was about to happen. Indeed, a new Park-and-Ride car park had been built at the Bradley Lane stop that opened at the beginning of February with spaces for 196 cars. New destination screens had been installed on platforms at stops across the system. The westward extension had opened to the Library and track on the Wolverhampton Station extension was being laid. The Metro was getting ready for extra passengers attracted by the new extensions.

There was an example of selfishness in February when a van driver parked his van in Corporation Street outside Poundland, blocking the path of trams running in the city centre. The driver had parked on the pavement, partially across the tram track and preventing trams from passing his van. When questioned by police the driver said he had just popped into a shop for ten minutes. Police stated that there are clear no parking signs and added that the motorist would be prosecuted for causing an unnecessary obstruction.

Work on the 11km long extension to Brierly Hill began in February 2020 with the removal of the central reservation of the A459 at Castle Hill, Dudley. The extension, that will cost £1.5 billion, was described as "not only supporting the re-generation of areas like Dudley town centre but offer people here vastly improved links to jobs and opportunities in the wider West Midlands and beyond". One objective of the new line is to provide a link between Dudley and the new High Speed 2 hub at Curzon Street. It is planned to open the route in 2023.

Early in the year there was news of a virus that had affected people in China. At first people in Europe were fairly relaxed about the news. However, in a few weeks it became clear that the world was in the grip of a pandemic, with country after country being affected. The first case in Britain was found towards the end of February. People were falling seriously ill and dying as a result of the virus. While the medical profession and hospitals were working hard treating patients and searching for a vaccination, Governments were taking action to ban all but essential journeys and events normally attracting crowds were prohibited. Only shops with essential items, such as grocers, supermarkets and chemists were allowed to open.

In the West Midlands, from Friday 3 March, all tram and bus journeys were made free for NHS staff going to or from duty on production of their NHS Staff Pass. West Midlands Mayor Andy Street said: "We want to do as much as we can to support our NHS workers at this difficult time, and I am delighted that our bus companies and the Midland Metro have stepped up to offer free services. The Tramway said that this was just a small way in which they can help all those people who, while many of us are safely staying at home, are going into busy hospitals to help save lives."

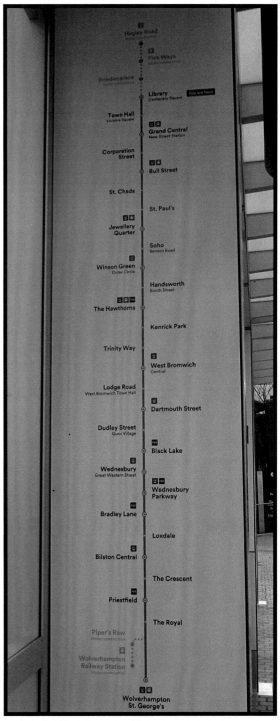

The Metro map at the Library stop. It shows the extension to Edgbaston.

93

Tramcar number 27 at the Library temporary terminus. Immediately behind the tram is the very distinctive exterior of the city library while to the left is the Birmingham Rep. Theatre. This shows the unique feature of this extension to the Metro, the absence of an overhead power supply.

The spread of the virus was such that in March the Government had to take action. In England on 20 March non-essential public areas such as schools, theatres and restaurants (though take-away meals could be sold) were closed and three days later a national lockdown was declared. In April the lockdown continued with the Prime Minister being admitted to hospital for intensive care. Outdoor events attracting crowds were banned. In May the restrictions were eased, with the direction "stay at home" changing to "stay alert". Garden centres and golf courses were allowed to open. Then on 23 March the Prime Minister announced that Britain would be in lock-down. People were told to stay at home and only go out if their work was essential (that included public transport to enable hospital staff to get to work); or to buy food and necessities; or for exercise. Most people followed the advice to stay home and not use public transport unless essential. The number of passengers on trams, buses and trains in the West Midlands urban area fell by 86%. The Metro started working a reduced timetable, with a twelve-minute headway. The Government told all non-essential workers to stay at home and all construction was paused, following guidelines introduced on the 23 March 2020. As a result, work on the Metro extension to Five Ways ceased as workers were furloughed.

On 27 March the Prime Minister announced that he had tested positive for Coronavirus and was self isolating. The press were told on 2 April that he was expected to end his self isolation the next day. The upbeat messages continued, while, in reality, his health deteriorated and on Sunday 5 April he was admitted to St Thomas' Hospital, where he was given oxygen. While he was fighting for breath, the official press briefing said that he was working on his red boxes. The next day he was transferred to the intensive care unit. The Foreign Secretary, Dominic Raab, took over as Deputy. On 9 April the Prime Minister was moved to a general ward. He discharged himself on Sunday 12 April saying that the NHS had saved his life "no question". He particularly paid tribute to the two nurses who cared for him.

On 30 March the tramway introduced a reduced temporary timetable. Up to 06.30 the service was to be every 15 min, then every 12 min to 20.00 then every 15 min. The Government revised the furlough on the 31 March and work on the Edgbaston phase of the extension resumed on the 3 April with a reduced number of workers (to enable social distancing to take place).

In March, the Government had announced emergency funding for buses and trains but nothing for tramways. The Midland Metro warned the Government that it was losing £1 million a month due to the fall in passenger numbers. The English tramway operators canvassed the Government for emergency funding to maintain their services. On 24 April the Department for Transport announced that it was working with the tramway networks in Greater Manchester, Sheffield, the West Midlands, Nottingham and Tyne and Wear to identify what support was necessary. On the 2 May the Government confirmed £30 million emergency funding for these five light rail systems announcing the following sums: Manchester £11.6 million; Tyne & Wear £8.6 million; Nottingham £3.7 million; West Midlands Metro £2.1 million (enough for about two months); Sheffield Supertram £1.3 million. In Blackpool bus route 1 covered most of the tram route and the tram service ceased at the end of March. The Transport Secretary said light rail played "a crucial role in getting NHS staff and emergency services workers to work". At the end of May the Government increased the emergency funding for all English tramways. The West Midlands received an additional £1.6 million. The Metro also increased the service level to a tram every 12 minutes in each direction up to 06.30. In October a further £1.9 million was allocated.

The conversion of the whole fleet for battery operation was completed on 10 April 2020 when tram number 26 re-entered service. The impact of the Coronavirus outbreak had an unusual side effect on the Tramway. The front section of each tramcar had been taped off for the use of Metro staff only. This ensured that staff travelling on the tram had an "isolated" area to minimise the likelihood of catching the virus from other passengers. In October a further £1.9 million was allocated by the Government.

Car 23 turning into Stephenson Street heading for the Grand Central stop (New Street Station) .

The impact of Coronavirus regulations had an adverse effect on Metro passenger numbers. For the first 17 years the annual passenger numbers were fairly level at around 5 million. Then on 2 May 2016, with the opening of the extension to New Street Station there was an increase in numbers to 6.2 million in 2016/17, as people could see trams running in Birmingham streets. These dropped slightly to 5.7 million in 2017/18, but increased to 8.3 million in 2018/19, an increase of 65% (June 2018 had seen a change in the operator and not for profit management). With the opening of the extension to Centenary Square, the year 2019/20 carried 8 million passengers. From March 2020 the Coronavirus restrictions impacted passenger numbers. The 2019/20 figure included the seven days when everyone was advised to stay at home, followed by eight days of the first self-isolation three-week period (making 15 days out of the full year). The total vehicle mileage for 2019/20 was 1.2 million, up 8.2% on the previous year. The number of passenger journeys fell 2.8% to 8 million while revenue rose by 3.8% to £11.3 million (€12.5 million). This is likely to have been the result of a fare increase of 0.7% on 8 December and the system expanding by two stops (Town Hall and Centenary Square) on 11 December.

In May the restrictions were eased, with the direction "stay at home" changing to "stay alert". Garden centres and golf courses were allowed to open. In June Premier League football resumed, but without the public being allowed in grounds. Non-essential shops were allowed to open as were pubs, cafes and restaurants. August saw a move towards more normality for most people. In September the "rule of six" was introduced where no more than six people could meet and all hospitality was subject to a 10.00pm curfew. In October the number of coronavirus cases rose sharply and restrictions were reintroduced. The Government introduced a tier system with three levels, having increasing restrictions. On 31 October a second national lock-down was announced that lasted from 6 November to 2 December. In December pubs could serve alcohol, but only with a substantial meal and families could only mix in outdoor areas. A new, tighter, level 4 was introduced. Families were told not to mix at Christmas. Astrazeneca and Pfizer vaccines were approved for use. In January a new lock-down came into effect with effectively no socialising with anyone outside a household. Non-essential shops were closed including pubs, restaurants and cafes. Schools were closed except for children of key workers. February saw the Government introduce 10 day quarantine in isolation hotels for people entering Britain from countries "red listed" due to the virus. In March the roadmap out of lockdown began. On 8 March schools reopened. Then on 29 March the rule of six returns, the stay at home and remaining in your locality rules are dropped and people can join outdoor organised sport. On 12 April non essential shops open and can stay open until 10.00pm. Pubs and restaurants can open but only outside, but no requirement to serve drinks only with meals. From 17 May groups of six people from two households can meet indoors.

The Government announced that, from 15 June, the wearing of face masks was compulsory on all public transport journeys. This was implemented by West Midlands Metro. Initially the approach to passengers was "engage, explain, educate and enforce." However, it was soon found that a stricter approach was required and passengers refusing to wear a face covering were ejected from the tram after their name and address was taken pending a Fixed Penalty Notice. This approach started on 29th June and by 9th July 533 passengers had been directed to leave public transport in the West Midlands. This included three fixed penalty notices and one person being arrested.

Car 25 climbs the hill up Colmore Circus Queensway to enter Bull Street. The steps on the right lead up to the entrance to Snow Hill Station.

Above: The end doors of each tramcar were reserved for staff travelling on the system, in order to give them some protection when they were moving about the system.

In order to encourage people to maintain social distancing seats were labelled to show the safe distances. Once lock-down was implemented there was a massive decline in the numbers of people travelling. Only essential travel was allowed. Face masks were compulsory in all public transport. vehicles.

Stay Safe
Stay Apart

We're working hard to keep **everyone** safe.

 Please wear a face covering

 Keep space between yourself and others

 Carry hand sanitiser and wash your hands before and after travelling

 Allow others to disembark before getting on any transport

 Pay for your ticket in advance or use contactless where possible

Thank you for supporting our efforts.
Enjoy your journey.

A campaign to inform the public of extra precautions necessary to safeguard each other was publicised by the West Midlands Network. Posters informing the public what they could do to help were distributed to all public transport operators.

Track laying in Broad Street approaching Five Ways roundabout. Work occupies most of the road, leaving a single one way carriageway for other road traffic.

In June work began on the £450 million 11 km long Wednesbury to Brierley Hill extension that was to connect to the existing Metro route to Birmingham centre. A second extension was started to connect the current Metro route to the High Speed 2 station at Curzon Street (due for completion 2023). West Midlands Mayor Andy Street welcomed the progress and said. "The Wednesbury to Brierley Hill Metro extension is a brilliant scheme for the Black Country, and I am determined we press ahead to help provide some economic certainty in the wake of the Coronavirus pandemic. I know the teams involved in the project have been busy throughout the crisis with design work and utility works in Dudley, so it's great that those living in Sandwell can see this project getting underway in their area too."

One of the less attractive aspects of public transport occurred in July 2020 when the British Transport Police published images of a male they wanted to interview in regard to reports of a series of public decency outrages occurring at different Metro stops between September 2019 and March 2020. There was no subsequent publicity as to whether the individual had been apprehended or not.

TABLE 1
COMPARISON OF PASSENGER MILES SINCE OPENING

Passenger journeys by financial year					
Year	Number of Passenger Journeys	Year	Number of Passenger Journeys	Year	Number of Passenger Journeys
1999/00	4.8 million	2006/07	4.9 million	2013/14	4.7 million
2000/01	5.4 million	2007/08	4.8 million	2014/15	4.4 million
2001/02	4.8 million	2008/09	4.7 million	2015/16	4.8 million
2002/03	4.9 million	2009/10	4.7 million	2016/17	6.2 million
2003/04	5.1 million	2010/11	4.8 million	2017/18	5.7 million
2004/05	5.0 million	2011/12	4.9 million	2018/19	8.3 million
2005/06	5.1 million	2012/13	4.8 million	2019/20	8.0 million

Department of Transport figures.

The Tramway announced in August that there had been a steady increase in the number of people using the service throughout the month, and it was likely to continue. To meet this demand the number of services were increased to the pre-pandemic levels from Tuesday 1 September with trams up to every 6 minutes on weekdays and 10 minutes at weekends. The Tramway stressed that it was important that everyone continue to follow government advice, maintaining social distancing and wear face coverings over the mouth and nose while using the Tramway. If possible people should plan their journey and choose a quieter time to travel. The Government were anticipating a reduction in the numbers of people being in-fected, as there was considerable pressure on hospitals.

The hoped-for continuing reduction in the numbers of people being infected did not occur. Instead there was a sharp rise in September leading to Local Covid Alert Levels being implemented in England. These were "Medium", "High" and "Very High" each with more severe restrictions than the previous level. Then the Government introduced further new restrictions on 5 November 2020 which effectively meant that most people were under strict lock-down rules and had to stay at home most of the time.

The Coronavirus outbreak did not stop the continued conflict between the trams and other road users. Around 7.20am on 5 November there was a collision between a tram and a Renault Clio on the Bilston Road. The car, with a driver and passenger, was crushed between the tram and a lamppost. Thankfully the people in the car were not seriously injured, while no passengers in the tram were harmed. Services between The Royal and St Georges were suspended while the vehicles were cleared from the scene.

There was a major step towards combating the virus on 8 December 2020 when the first member of the public in Britain was given the first inoculation against the infection. It took until after Christmas before the full inoculation programme was started.

In December 2020 the Metro advertised a number of jobs as part of the preparation for opening the exten-sions from 2021 Three types of post were identified. These being "Driver Customer Representative"; "Maintenance Technician" and "Infrastructure Maintenance Manager" all based at Wednesbury Depot.

Also in December, builders working on the Dudley extension of the Metro discovered an ancient well in Flood Street car park. Councillor Ian Kettle, cabinet member for regeneration and enterprise at Dudley Council, said: "Dudley has a long and fascinating history, and it is always exciting to discover items of historical interest. The unearthing of the well provides a very interesting look at Dudley in days-gone-by at a time when so much work is taking place to transform the Borough through new developments and technological advances, including the Metro."

The Bull Street tram stop showing that a ten minute service is in operation, but with no customers.

Car 36 arriving at the Library temporary terminus with the Town Hall and Hall of Memory.

Christmas was approaching and people were making plans for family celebrations. However, the spread of Covid was speeding up and the Government, that had been hinting that there could be an easing of re-strictions to allow family members to meet, now discouraged any idea of meeting. Travelling distances was discouraged, with police turning people back. A very restricted meeting within families was allowed, but only for Christmas Day and Boxing Day. The three tier system was expanded to four tiers, the extra tier being even more restrictive (tier five was introduced soon after, indicating that the health service was in danger of being overwhelmed). The descriptions were changed to Medium Alert; High Alert; Very High Alert; Stay at Home. Apart from the Isles of Scilly, the whole of England was in either level 4 or level 3. A rigid lockdown started in the New Year. The hospitality sector was shut down, as were shops selling non essential items. The following Government rules were introduced. People were only allowed out of their home to shop for essentials, go to work or to volunteer or provide charitable services if it could not be done at home, exercise (with their household or support bubble) once a day and within their local area. People could also seek medical assistance, leave their house to avoid injury, illness or risk of harm or to go to school or other education or childcare. This was introduced with little warning creating difficulties at schools and many did not open, but provided lessons via computer. In addition anyone testing positive for Covid 19 or who had been in contact with someone testing positive must isolate for ten days. Later most schools closed due to the pandemic. These rules applied to England and began in January and lasted until 8 March when a programme of gradual easing of restrictions began. The programme was to last until 21 June when the last restrictions were lifted, though there was a warning that if the number of Covid 19 cases rose, the programme would change and restrictions could be extended or reintroduced. This indeed did happen and the restrictions continued until 19 July 2021.

The 28 April 2021 saw the delivery of the first of the new tramcars that had been ordered in October 2019. Number 39 arrived as a complete unit on the back of a very long low loader. It was similar in design to the previous Urbs 3 trams from CAF. Number 40 arrived on 26 May. A total of 21 tramcars had been ordered with eight for delivery in 2021 and a further thirteen scheduled for delivery in 2023 to meet the demands of the Brierley Hill and Eastside extensions. The plan was that of the initial eight cars, five would enter service later in 2021 to meet the extra needs when the new extensions in Birmingham and Wolverhampton open. As detailed later, repairs to the Urbis 3 stock in early 2022 meant they were supplemented by all eight new trams in order to allow the service to be re-opened. The new trams are similar to those delivered in 2014, with slight modifications. They will all have roof mounted batteries to enable operation over the catenary-free sections of track.

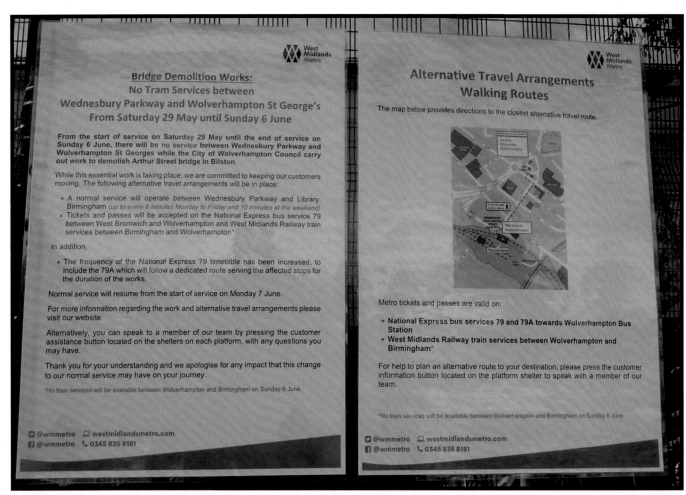

Notices pinned up at Wednesbury Great Western Street informing passengers that between 29 May and 6 June inclusive there would be no tram service between Wednesbury Parkway and Wolverhampton, instead tickets could be used on identified bus routes and railway services. There were similar notices at all other stops.

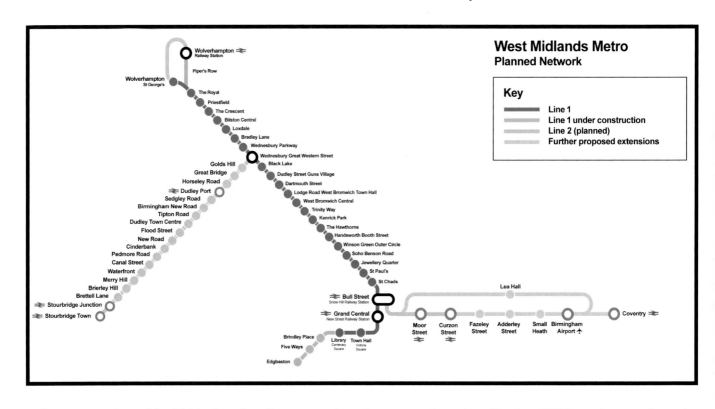

A map produced in 2021 showing the current and proposed routes. During 2021 work was almost complete on the Wolverhampton Station and Five Ways extensions and work had started on the Brindley Lane and Coventry Street routes.

Tram number 35 on the catenary-free section of the line outside the Library.

The old Arthur Street road bridge in Bilston (between Bilston Central and The Crescent stops) had been closed to road vehicle traffic for twenty years. A replacement footbridge was built above the old bridge. Though not used, the old bridge was eventually declared "unsafe" and arrangements were set in motion to demolish it leaving just the new footbridge. In order to enable the work to take place the Tramway was closed between Wednesbury Parkway and Wolverhampton city centre from 29 May 2021, coinciding with schools half term. Arrangements had been made to enable passengers to use tram tickets and passes on National Express bus service route 79 (with additional short working buses on special route 79A) and West Midlands railway services between Birmingham and Wolverhampton. An alternative pedestrian route was marked to enable the public to walk cross the Tramway. These arrangements lasted until and including 6 June when the Metro recommenced the full scheduled service on 7 June. Intending passengers could choose the Metro or a substitute between Library and Wednesbury Parkway and the substitutes between Parkway and Wolverhampton. To assist them, staff were available at the tram stops to explain the temporary arrangements and notices were displayed at all the stops.

Sunday 6 June 2021 also saw the closure of Lower Bull Street to all through traffic. This was to enable pointwork to be installed for the East Side route. Initially the new route would be to Albert Street, the HS2 Interchange, Curzon Street and Digbeth High Street. Later extensions will take the route to Birmingham Airport and the NEC. The Metro announced that the service between Bull Street and The Library would cease while the junction was being built. It was anticipated that the service to Centenary Square (the Library) and possibly Five Ways, would commence by the autumn, once Lower Bull Street had reopened. Initially the Eastside extension would terminate at Deritend High Street with stops at Albert Street, New Canal Street and Meriden Street. Opening of the line will be linked to the completion of the HS2 station.

There was a repeat of problems with the overhead in the St Pauls area. On 9 June 2021 at around midday the overhead was damaged and the service was terminated at Winson Green and passengers were advised that their tickets would be valid on bus route 74. There had been a number of issues regarding this section of overhead, indeed there had been a similar issue earlier in the year. A spokesman said "Due to damage to the overhead lines, trams are unable to stop between Library at Centenary Square and Winson Green". The line reopened around 19.00 the same evening.

There was some most unwelcome news from CAF when the Metro management were informed that a tramcar under routine maintenance was discovered to have cracks that appeared in the underframe structure at either end of the tram. CAF was unable to reassure the Metro that the cracks did not represent a safety issue if the tramway continued to operate. Therefore, as a precautionary measure, the service ceased in the morning of Friday 11 June. The tramway issued a statement: "Following maintenance checks, CAF, the manufacturer of the Urbos 3 trams used on the West Midlands Metro, has informed us of a fault affecting a small number of our trams. As a result of their findings, we have made the decision to remove the whole fleet from service to allow all trams to be inspected. At no point has customer or staff safety been compromised. This is a temporary and precautionary measure we have taken to ensure the service can continue to run safely and efficiently in the future."

"We are currently working alongside CAF to restore service as soon as possible. We are sorry for the inconvenience this will cause. Alternative services are detailed below and arrangements are in place to ensure our customers are still able to travel safely and reliably around the region. All Metro tickets will be valid on bus service 79 between Wolverhampton – West Bromwich and Birmingham. Passengers can also use train services between Birmingham Snow Hill, the Jewellery Quarter and The Hawthorns as well as train services between Wolverhampton and Birmingham New Street. "The manufacturer has already started inspections on the fleet of trams and the Metro engineering team are working closely with them so that services can resume as quickly as possible. We will keep customers fully updated via our website and social media channels."

The tramway immediately started inspections of the trams, which continued through the weekend. On Monday a decision was able to be made regarding the resumption of services. A reduced ten minutes (compared to the usual six to eight minutes) service commenced first thing Tuesday morning, 15 June. Due to a reduced number of available trams the service terminated in Bull Street. A spokesman said "We will increase the frequency of our service as the affected trams are repaired and return to service. We are sorry for the inconvenience that the service suspension has caused. Thank you for your continued understanding while we work hard to resume a full service as soon as possible." The tramway did not identify which trams or how many were affected. As a precautionary measure a regime of daily inspections was introduced. The temporary terminus at Bull Street enabled work to start on the junction with the new Eastside route (due to be opened in 2023). The short working did not last long as the full route to the Library was reopened on Sunday 20 June, though the reduced service continued due to trams still under repairs.

At the Library stop the notices informing intending travellers of the closure of part of the tramway and telling them of the alternative arrangements. Similar notices were displayed at every stop.

However, there was more unfortunate news when at 05.00 on Saturday 26 June, it was reported that the tramway overhead had suffered damage. Service on the northern section of the line was halted meaning no trams ran between Wednesbury Parkway and the terminus at Wolverhampton St Georges. It was announced that tram tickets were accepted on bus route 79 and train services between Birmingham and Wolverhampton. The trams continued to run a ten minute service between the Library and Wednesbury Parkway. Then at around midday a single line shuttle service was introduced between Wednesbury Parkway and Wolverhampton. This ceased on Sunday 27 June to enable repair work to take place. The whole route was worked from Monday 28, with services ending around midnight to allow repair work to continue during the nights. A resumption of a full service was announced early morning on Tuesday 29 June. It is not known why the Metro has had more than its fair share of overhead line problems.

Trams numbers 22 and 35 at Wednesbury Great Western Street, alongside the depot. This was taken in June 2021 during the short working to enable the demolition of the unsafe, disused Arthur Street bridge. This was the first of many interruptions during June and July

A Government scandal broke on the weekend of 26/27 June when the Daily Mirror printed a photograph of Matt Hancock (Secretary of State for Health and Social Care) and a member of his staff in an embrace (in contravention of Covid rules). This led to his resignation and he was replaced by Sajid Javid on 28 June. The new Health Secretary said his immediate priority was to ease covid restrictions as soon as possible. However, a day later the Prime Minister confirmed that the previously announced date of 19 July 2021 for the easing of social distancing rules would continue to apply, including the rules applying to public transport.

The planned extension of the Tramway took another step forward on 6 July with the start of work in Lower Bull Street for the Eastside extension in preparation for the construction of the 1.7km extension to the HS2 station at Curzon Street and on to Digbeth High Street. The proposals include running a section of the new route as a catenary free operation.

At the end of June the Tramway announced that from 25 July the Tramway would temporarily terminate at Bull Street. This was to take advantage of the closure required to construct the link to the Eastside extension which would also enable the rails in Corporation Street through to Grand Central to be replaced. The Tramway reported that the new closure was required due to track alignment issues that needed rectification, though only five years old. This can be compared to the renewal of rails in 2017 on the road to Wolverhampton that had a life of eighteen years. Like the Corporation Street track the Wolverhampton road was shared with other road traffic. However, there were issues with the track in Corporation Street just before opening, though no detailed explanation was given for the extra work carried out. Nor has it been detailed why the rails in this part of the tramway have needed replacement so soon. However, there is an indication in ITV News Web Page for 17 May 2016. It reported that this was the third delay in the opening date and "This time it is because safety testing of the trams on the new lines found the rails are not per-fectly level." It appeared that the rails had been laid with superelevation on the curves, when the tops of the rails should have been level with each other. The inspectorate required this to be remedied, which was done by grinding a significant section off the tops of the outer rails, drastically reducing the life expectancy. Phil Hewitt, Centro's Midland Metro Programme Director was reported as saying: "It is bitterly disappointing as everything else is in place and ready to go but, as we have said right from the start, safety is paramount. A stringent testing programme has identified minor anomalies in some of the track alignment which need to be addressed. These are exactly the sort of issues the tests were designed to identify. However remedial work is relatively straightforward. Once that is complete, on-street driver training can begin and we will soon have passenger services running."

The current remedial work in Corporation Street was expected to last approximately three months. The opening of the new line to Edgbaston is now expected to be December. Many shop keepers in Corporation Street and Stephenson Street were unhappy as they had only just reopened for three weeks after six months of lock-down. Now they were faced with no trams passing their shops and both streets being dug up from 25 July. To add to their difficulties the Tramway was unable to give any firm date when the roads would reopen. The Midland Metro Alliance, which did not build the stretch that it is replacing, said: "The cost of the work was a matter for other parties", without specifying who they might be.

The announcement about the changes was made on the web site:

"**Changes to normal service from 24 July**

From Saturday 24 July, there will be changes to our normal services while work is carried out to tie-in the existing track to the Birmingham Eastside Extension which will connect Metro services with Digbeth and the new HS2 station at Curzon Street. There will also be track replacement work taking place on Corporation Street at the same time.

There will be the following changes to our normal timetable to allow this work to be completed:
- On Saturday 24 July, trams will terminate at St Chads from 21:30 until the end of service
- On Sunday 25 July, trams will terminate at St Chads from 19:00 until the end of service
- From Monday 26 July until October 2021, trams will operate between Wolverhampton St George's and Bull Street only. There will be no services between Bull Street and Library.

Alternative travel arrangements will be provided for the duration of the work, which is due to be completed in October."
We are sorry for any disruption to your journey caused by this essential work.
Thank you for your understanding while the work to deliver our Metro extensions takes place."

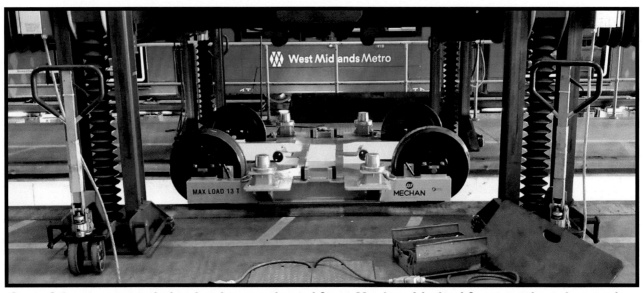

One of the accommodation bogies purchased from Mechan Limited for use when the service bogies are removed for maintenance. Photo Mechan Limited.

On 1 July it was announced that the Metro had purchased three accommodation bogies from Mechan Limited, manufacturer of specialist lifting equipment for rail workshops. The bogies are for use under trams that have had their bogies removed for maintenance or repair. They were specifically designed for the Urbos 3 tramcars. Mechan Limited said that the accommodation bogies "will enable a slicker and safer bogie refurbishment programme."

The Mayor of the West Midlands, Andy Street, announced on 5 July that wearing facemasks on the West Midlands Metro or local bus services would no longer be compulsory after July 19. He said he would wear a face mask voluntarily if he was on a busy bus. This announcement was in anticipation of an announcement by the Prime Minister that regional transport authorities would be free to set their own rules. The Mayor said " If the Government removes the mandatory requirement to wear face coverings on public transport from July 19, as has been widely reported, then Transport for West Midlands will implement this guidance across the region's network. If this were to be the new guidance then we would want passengers to follow a common sense approach, using their own judgement as to when it might be appropriate to wear a face covering and when not. For example I know personally that if I'm on a busy bus sat next to someone who could be a bit more vulnerable then I'll wear one, but perhaps if I'm on a very empty train carriage I may not. As part of this personal responsibility we would want residents to be mindful of rising Covid-rates across the West Midlands, and try and avoid passing on the virus inadvertently."

A Government spokesman said that after 19 July transport operators still have the power to make masks compulsory, as part of what's called Conditions of Carriage and this is what the Mayor of London has said he would do. The West Midlands Combined Authority, chaired by the Mayor, Andy Street, said the region would stick with the new rules as set out by Boris Johnson, in order to provide "one clear message" to travellers, meaning that masks will be encouraged, but optional.

The lifts at Bilston Central and Lodge Road stops were closed on 7 July 2021 to allow upgrading work to be undertaken in order to make their operation more reliable. Notices informed the public that the lifts would be out of order until September. Notices informed the public that during the work there would be no step-free access at Bilston Central and advised passengers needing to use a lift to take bus route 79 to travel to the Crescent stop, using their tickets and passes. At Lodge Road passengers were advised that there was a ramp at the Lodge Road and Victoria Street entrance. The work was expected to last until September 2021.

At midnight on 18/19 July, in England, crowds gathered in pubs and night clubs to celebrate the ending of Covid restrictions, despite the number of cases of people catching the virus having risen to around 50,000 a day and the cumulative total to 5.5M. The Department for Health and Social Care could not provide an exact total for the number of people currently self-isolating. However, estimates were published that gave figures of between 1.6M and 2M people daily were self isolating by the time restrictions ceased.

However, things were far from clear. For example, the big supermarkets continued to rule that all customers, unless exempt, had to wear face masks. The Mayor of London said that all passengers on public transport in the city had to wear masks, while the television news showed pictures of crowds entering pubs and night clubs at midnight on 18 July when social distancing was no longer compulsory. At the same time the numbers contracting Covid rose dramatically with some 45,000 new cases each day. As if to emphasis the situation the Health Secretary was diagnosed with Covid on Saturday 17 July having met with the Prime Minister and the Chancellor of the Exchequer the previous day. This meant that all three had to self isolate for ten days. On Monday 19 July the two contacts said they were being included in an experimental trial that allowed them to continue contacting others.

In July 2021 the track had been laid in Broad Street, but no trams had ventured onto the rails. Here the tramway goes under the pedestrian bridge between the Hyatt Hotel and the International Convention Centre. The temporary stop at the Library is behind the photographer

The meeting of Corporation Street and Bull Street where the junction to the Eastside route will be built in summer 2021. Preparatory work has already started.

The reaction from the tens of thousands forced to self isolate was rapid and vociferous. Within two hours the Prime Minister and Chancellor changed their minds and said they were self isolating. Two days later on 21 July the Leader of the Opposi-tion confirmed that he was self isolating as one of his children had been confirmed as having Covid. Not a propitious start to coming out of Covid restrictions.

There was a further disruption to the tram service on the evening of 22 July, when all tram services were halted between Birmingham Library and Wolverhampton St Georges, due to damage to the overhead lines. Once again tickets were accepted on bus routes 74 and 79, West Midlands Railway and Avanti Coast Services. The past week has not been a happy one for the Metro with overhead issues interrupting services on three occasions. This is the third piece of overhead damage that the Metro has seen in less than a week with disruption on 17/18 July and again on 19 July with repairs to this second area of damage having only being completed to enable services to run from the start of Tuesday 20 July, only to be halted again on 22 July. The Birmingham Mail reported frustrations being felt by passengers. One was reported as saying "Why do I pay for a Metro monthly pass and spend most of the time on the bus?! Unacceptable really."

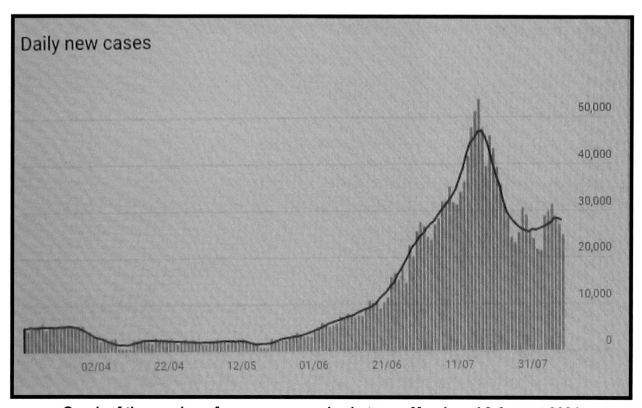

Graph of the number of new cases per day between March and 8 August 2021.

The temporary terminus at the Library became unused when the tramway service was cut short to Bull Street while work on the Eastside junction and re-laying track in Corporation Street and Stephenson Street was in progress. It was due to re-open with the new track to Edgbaston in December 2021. However the line to the Library did not open until February 2022.

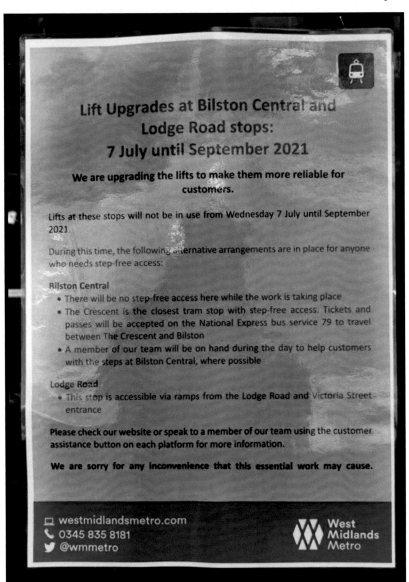

Notices were placed at all stops informing the public of work being undertaken on the lifts at Bilston Central and Lodge Road stops, which meant there was no access by lift at Bilston Central while the work was being undertaken.

Work on the removal and relaying tracks in Corporation and New Streets and laying the pointwork for the new route to the HS2 station began on Sunday 25 July and immediately raised complaints from people living in the area. Residents in the area soon complained due to loud bangs though the night waking them up. In response to their complaints, Midland Metro Alliance (MMA) apologised for 'any inconvenience' caused by the works. A spokesman said "A dedicated line has been set up for anyone who has any questions or concerns about the works and I would urge them to contact 07376 273079 or email communications@metroalliance.co.uk where a member of our Engagement Team will be available to speak to them at any time during the day or night.". Trams terminated at Bull Street and in order to enable the trackwork to take place safely the overhead power was switched off beyond St Chads stop. So trams would lower their pantograph at St Chads and proceed to Bull Street stop using battery power.

July also saw the launch of the West Midlands Metro Training Academy. Based at the Wednesbury depot by the Great Western Street tram stop it is part of a campaign to fill an anticipated 160 new jobs created by the expansion of the network with the extensions to Wolverhampton Station and Edgbaston due to open in December 2021. The Training Academy was established to give the new recruits the skills they need and to develop the careers of existing workers. Sophie Allison, MML Commercial Director, said: "As we look forward to the opening of new routes, our workforce is expected to expand by more than 70 per cent. Our focus is now on recruiting talented people from the communities we serve, and ensuring the Metro remains a great place to work where everyone is treated with respect and feels valued and cared for. At the same time, the West Midlands Metro Academy will help ensure both new and existing members of the team continue to deliver the best possible service to customers. The customer is at the heart of everything we do, and the only way we can deliver the high standards they deserve is by investing in the people who deliver the service everyday."

A new concern was raised by the Birmingham Mail newspaper and its online website BirminghamLive on 9 August. It reported that the four new tram stops in Broad Street, due to open to the public later in the year were in, its view, a potential hazard. The surface of the stop area is 300mm (11.5 inches) higher than the road surface, in order to align with the floor of the tramcar. This is around twice the height of a standard pavement curb. The spokesman for Midland Metro Alliance said "The Midland Metro Alliance consulted with local accessibility groups regarding the proposals, which resulted in the development and inclusion of additional tactile paving around the international symbol of access to improve accessibility for less abled users." Sarah Gayton, a shared spaces safety campaigner for the

Sign on the depot wall identifying it as the site of the Metro Training Academy

National Federation of the Blind of the UK, told BirminghamLive: "Having a kerb that deep directly outside of a pub is potentially asking for trouble. The tactile pavement and guide dog would help a blind or partially sighted person to avoid it. But I've been out at night investigating various spaces in terms of e-scooter users riding around. I've seen people who've had a drink in Birmingham city centre not having a clue what they are doing. When people have had a drink in a busy area there can be lots of excitement and lads pushing each other. So 12 inches is a significant drop in a potentially hazardous location." Surely getting intoxicated to that extent is a self inflicted hazard, as well as being socially unacceptable. Additionally, all the metro tram stops have this design and there have been no reports of injuries to the public caused by tripping when stepping off the platform, though there was a case of a member of the public so inebriated that he lay on the track and went to sleep.

The start of the reduction of restrictions was encouraging with the number of daily new cases falling from above 46,000 to 23,000 in the first seven days. But then the numbers increased over the next two days to over 30,000 a day, falling back to 21,000 a day by 3 August, then up again on 4 August to 28,000. Instead, the number of new cases recorded each day started to fall. Epidemiologists have said that the end of the Euro 2020 soccer championship and school summer holidays might have helped reduce the spread of the virus, as well as cautious behaviour in the population. Instead, the number of new cases recorded each day started to fall. Epidemiologists have said that the drop in numbers could be associated with the end of the Euro 2020 soccer championship and school summer holidays as well as the as the cautious behaviour in the population.

The final work on the extension to Wolverhampton Station began in August. The line had been built from the new junction just before the St Georges stop to Railway Drive, the approach road to the railway station. The final few yards had been left until work on the new station building was completed. Work on the terminus recommenced at the beginning of August and it is planned that the tram service on the new extension would open in 2021.

Just over a week later the local paper returned to Broad Street, this time with the complaints of cycle riders. In order to increase the width of the pavements for pedestrians the road was narrowed and parts were made particularly narrow. The Council said its policy was "to ensure everyone has a safe, viable and sustainable transport option." A spokesperson for the Council added: "We are working hard to ensure that Birmingham's highways network is re-balanced to provide everyone with safe and reliable transport options. We cannot provide segregated cycle tracks everywhere, and whilst we have widened the footways on Broad Street there are certain constraints in delivering the public transport improvements, that means it is impractical to fully accommodate cycling along the stretch. Not-withstanding the significant environmental enhancements made to the street-scene by the project and improved pedestrian facilities, there are limitations on where cycles, pedestrians and the requisite public transport infrastructure can be safely reconciled in shared use. Particularly in the high footfall entertainments areas like Broad Street, where we look forward to a resurgence in the vibrant hospitality sector as the city recovers from the Covid-19 pandemic. We would advise that the tram stops prevent safe cycling between the rail and the kerb. As a result the final scheme will necessarily prevent cycling between Sheepcote St and Berkley Street, and at the Five Ways underpass. Cyclists are still permitted to use the strip between the rail and the kerb along the rest of the track but should proceed with caution when crossing the rails, and consider dismounting to do so. For the tram stop near Ryland Street, an alternative route via Ryland St, Grosvenor Street West and Sheepcote Street is available to avoid passing the tram stop. There are also several pedestrian crossings along the length of the track. As a council, we are committed to ensuring walking and cycling are viable transport options across the city and continue to work with our partners to improve cycling infrastructure. We want to ensure that everyone has a safe, viable and sustainable transport option but this doesn't happen overnight. We remain committed to improving the city centre to deliver a fully integrated transport network. Our City Centre Segments scheme is currently open for public consultation, which will see the city centre divided into a number of segments and movement between the segments enhanced for public transport, pedestrians, and cyclists."

It seems that relationships with their future customers was not improved during the work relaying the tram track along Corporation Street and Stephenson Street; and the laying of the new junction. The work appeared to create unhappiness with the people of Birmingham. During week seven of the disruption the tramway felt it necessary to place notices on the fencing around the work areas. They informed the public: - "K**P !T C!V!L WITH OUR STAFF Our staff have the right to work in a safe environment and are here to help you. We will not tolerate violence, physical aggression or verbal abuse towards our staff." Presumably the use of asterixis and exclamation marks was an attempt to introduce a jocular approach.

On 17 September the West Midlands Combined Authority approved a bid to the Government to improve transport in the region. These included new Metro routes. An extension from Five Ways along the Hagley Road at least as far as Bearwood; a connection between Wolverhampton and New Cross Hospital; another connection between Wolverhampton and New Cross Hospital; a route between Wednesbury to Walsall and another between Brierley Hill and Stourbridge. There is also a bid for funding the refurbishment of the original Birmingham to Wolverhampton line – including an upgrade of overhead cables and "modernisation of power supply". Funding over a five year period was agreed by the Government's City Region Sustainable Transport Settlement (CRSTS) Fund.

There was a small celebration outside Wolverhampton Railway Station on 20 September 2021 when Andy Street, Mayor of West Midlands and Councillor Stephen Simkins, Deputy Leader of Wolverhampton Council celebrated the installation of the final section of track leading to the entrance to the Station. The tramway plans to open the extension before the end of the year or early in 2022.

The final yards of the extension to the new frontage of Wolverhampton Railway Station were laid in September 2021 ready for opening later in the year or early 2022. Photo Midland Metro Alliance.

In September, Dudley Council was granted £96,000 by the Arts Council England to set up an 'Art Track: Metro Art Programme' for the design of art projects along the Metro track and at stops in Dudley Borough. There will be a competition for artists to design physical works, artistic residencies, community engagement programmes and there will be an opportunity for the public to see design proposals in an exhibition in Spring 2022. Councillor Simon Phipps, cabinet member for economic regeneration, said: "We are delighted to be successful in our Arts Council England application. This money will help to make the fantastic Metro development even more attractive and will be a welcome opportunity for local artists to get creative." The Mayor of the West Midlands and chair of the WMCA, Andy Street, said: "The Wednesbury to Brierley Hill Metro extension will be a game-changer for the Black Country as it will help to boost public transport whilst providing much-needed links to the existing rail and bus networks. Construction for this highly-anticipated route continues to move ahead at pace and it is great that, once open for passenger service, the area will be enhanced further with a selection of artwork."

As this history of the Tramway draws to a close the impact of the Coronavirus on all our lives has been be-yond our wildest imagination. Looking back, the last two years have been quite remarkable. There have been three lockdowns, when the population were required to stay at home, with only essential workers allowed to travel to work. All the other workers were either laid off or required to work at home. As previous-ly described this had a major impact on tramway passenger numbers as the table below illustrates.

WEST MIDLANDS METRO

COMPARISON OF STATISTICS BETWEEN YEARS 2019/2020 AND 2020/2021
(Department for Transport statistics)

Reduction in passenger journeys	58.4%
Reduction in vehicle miles	9.8%
Reduction in passenger revenue	52.1%

This gives a stark illustration of the impact of Coronavirus as the effect on 2019/2020 was just for one month, March 2020. The virus had a major impact on the whole of 2020/2021. Statistics for the reminder of 2021/2022 will not be available until mid 2022.

The Department for Transport also gave a breakdown of the reason for travelling, however, this covers all English tramways for the years 2012– 2019 inclusive:

Commuting	42%
Leisure	23%
Shopping	16%
Education	9%
Personal Business	5%
Business	4%
Other	2%

Chancellor Rishi Sunak announced in the Autumn Budget statement that the West Midlands has been awarded £1.05 billion for major transport improvements including bus and Metro schemes. The projects identified for receiving funding includes the completion of the 11km Wednesbury to Brierley Hill Metro extension. Mr Sunak said: "Great cities need great transport and that is why we're investing billions to improve connections in our city regions as we level up opportunities. There is no reason why somebody working in the North and Midlands should have to wait several times longer for their bus or train to arrive in the morning compared to a commuter in the capital. This transport revolution will help redress that imbalance as we modernise our local transport networks so they are fit for our great cities and those people who live and work in them."

Before bringing the story to a close there are still two more aspects to be mentioned. The proposals to open a Very Light Rail tramway in Coventry and bids for funding to reopen the rail passenger route from Stourbridge to Brierly Hill using a VLR system. These are explored in the next chapter.

The Hawthornes stop had new lifts installed in early 2021, replacing the original ones installed in 1995 when the rail station opened. Photo West Midlands Metro.

(From left to right) Sandeep Shingadia - Director of Development & Delivery at Transport for West Midlands, Darren Smith from TDI, Councillor Jim O'Boyle, James Kempston from NPAerospace, Professor Dave Greenwood from WMG, University of Warwick. Photo Coventry City Council/ William Hunt.

CHAPTER 9

Coventry Very Light Rail 2018/21
And Stourbridge Very Light Rail 2006-2022

Coventry Very Light Rail

The idea of developing a new concept in public tramways began in 2013 with the proposal to develop-ing a very light rail (VLR) innovation centre and rail line came to fruition by using part of the old track bed of the former Dudley railway station at Castle Hill. Two tracks had been proposed, one to be used for pilot testing VLR vehicles and the other for passenger services connecting to the national rail network (for the first time in over fifty years). This will provide connections to Birmingham City Centre, Dudley town centre, Dudley Zoo and the Black County Living museum. It was hoped to start work on the project in June 2014 with the construction of the innovation centre to begin in the second half of 2016. It was expected that there would be a five year research and construction period before services on the railway line would start.

The project was initially funded with £1.6m received by Revolution VLR in November 2013 from the Enabling Innovation Team (EIT) of the Rail Safety and Standards Board (RSSB) by participating in EIT's Radical Train challenge. The estimate for the overall cost of the development was £35M. Of this £4.5M had been allocated from the Black Country Local Enterprise Partnership's Growth Deal. It was anticipated that the remaining amount will be met through European funding, private sector investment and contributions by the Dudley Council.

Proposed ultra light rail vehicle designed by the Revolution VLR Consortium. It was publicised following a deal struck between Dudley Council and Warwick Manufacturing Group at the University of Warwick. Photo Revolution VLR Consortium.

The initial proposals were to use the Revolution VLR Consortium's hybrid propulsion technology which would be combined with a self-powered bogie and modular, composite bodyshell design. The Consortium consisted of (TDI (Europe) Ltd (Transport Design International), Unipart Rail Ltd, Warwick Manufacturing Group centre HVM Catapult, Trelleborg PPL Ltd, Allectra Ltd and GKN Land Systems) The project intended to use off-the-shelf components as much as possible to reduce manufacturing cost and improve reliability and maintenance. The bogies are driven by a unique, built in, series hybrid drivetrain with a clean diesel power driving electrically-driven bogies.

The idea took a step forward when Dudley Council and Warwick Manufacturing Group at the University of Warwick reached an agreement in 2014 to jointly build a trial line using very light rail vehicles. The initial proposals were to explore the use of very light rail trams powered by a series hybrid drivetrain built into the bogies (with clean diesel motors driving electrically-driven bogies).

In February 2015 the proposals were awarded £4.5M funding from The Black Country Local Enterprise Partnership's Growth Deal. The estimate of the total cost was £20M with the balance found from European funding, private sector investment and Dudley Council. The Centre would initially focus on prototype vehicle design and construction and also provide education, and research and development facilities to local businesses. The overall aim was to make Dudley and the Black Country the world's leading provider of low-carbon, very-lightweight railcars, utilising hybrid propulsion technology to transform the performance, cost and sustainability of light-rail-based passenger services.

At around the same time Councillors in Coventry had been following the development of tramways in Birmingham and Wolverhampton with interest and had suggested that their city could benefit from a similar service. However, there were doubts as to the financial viability of such an initiative, particularly as the West Midlands Metro had not reached the anticipated levels of ridership. However, the Midlands has a proud record of meeting challenges and this is no exception. Further constraints were that two of its major attractions are located out of town; in the north is the Ricoh football stadium and to the south is Warwick University. The Council investigated building a city tramway based on very light rail technology. The outline proposals include four circular routes, each starting in the city centre and radiating north, east, south and west. The first route will serve the railway station and Walsgrave Hospital with a target date for opening of 2025. It is being specifically designed to be compatible with the Midland Metro. It will have consistent operating systems and branding across the West Midlands area.

The driver's cab of the prototype tramcar. Photo Coventry City Council/William Hunt.

In January 2018 the partnership of Warwick Manufacturing Group (WMG) and Dudley Council submitted a planning application for the centre. This included building an access bridge between car parking and the centre. The building included meeting rooms, laboratories, teaching facilities, exhibition and conference space and a large engineering workshop. Research at the hub is aimed at reducing the weight and cost of railcars and track, enabling the creation of more affordable connections between suburban and rural areas and providing a cheaper alternative to heavy rail and traditional 'Metro' urban transport systems. This part of the project was estimated to cost nearly £25 million. The Black Country Local Enterprise Partnership provided the Dudley Council with a £18 million sum and a funding bid for the remaining £7 million was submitted to the Government.

In 2019 WMG agreed to collaborate with Transport Design International Ltd to develop the very light rail public transport system for Coventry. The project is led by Coventry City Council and Transport for West Midlands to develop a street running, rail-guided and battery powered people mover system. The project is funded with help from the Government's Local Growth Fund through the Coventry and Warwickshire Local Enterprise Partnership and West Midlands Combined Authority Devolution Deal (WMCA). The Local Growth Fund provided £2.46m for the first phase of the research work and design of the demonstrator vehicle, while the WMCA Devolution Deal contributed £12.2m to fund research and development activities to prove the VLR concept. Coventry City Council received £1.5m funding from WMCA to support the development of a cost-effective trackform. This is different from the initial, Dudley proposals, as it plans to use battery powered electric trams smaller than the initially advocated diesel hybrid power vehicles.

The objectives of the project were to include:-

1. Reducing Coventry transport carbon emissions, which currently amount to about 1/3 of the city's total greenhouse gas emissions;
2. Improve air quality by reducing the number of fossil-fuel vehicles on the roads;
3. Stimulate economic development and innovation within Coventry;
4. Make the city a more attractive place to live and work, to study and invest;
5. Encourage people to move away from owning their own car and using public transport (sometimes called Mobility as a Service or MaaS);
6. Providing an affordable alternative to conventional light rail systems, which due to cost can make business cases challenging.

Preparing the track bed ready for rail laying rails. Photo Dudley Metropolitan Borough Council. *Track laid in the tunnel. Photo Dudley Metropolitan Borough Council.*

Construction of the centre was expected to be completed in February 2022 and was promoted as having the aim of promoting development of the Very Light Rail industry and associated manufacturing in the Black Country. Their promotional material said "VLR offers a new, lower-cost, public transport solution that is set to transform the rail industry, providing integrated VLR systems as an alternative to heavy rail and traditional Metro transport." The VLR 2km test track will run between Castle Hill Bridge and Cinder Bank, with a test passenger platform located at the Cinder Bank end of the tracks. It will be used as a test bed for the Coventry VLR. The test track was completed in February 2021.

The aim is to develop a public transport system that has a very economic infrastructure, encourages the public to switch from using cars to public transport and does not pollute the streets. The ultimate aim is for the trams to be autonomous, not requiring a driver, and have been likened to the London Underground. NP Aerospace, of Foleshill, Coventry, was contracted in 2020 to assemble the first tramcar. For strength and lightness the body, designed to carry 56 passengers, is constructed from steel, aluminium and com-posite, with a carbon/polyethylene bumper and carbon/kevlar cab ends. The glazing is made from poly-carbonate (a recommendation following the Croydon accident). Like most trams the vehicle is bidirection-al. However, unlike most trams it uses battery traction, charging them at special places with technology used in electric buses. This eliminates the need for overhead cables.

The interior of the tram showing its clean and simple lines. Given that the initial proposals involve short passenger journeys, there are a limited numbers of seats, with more standing accommodation available. The tram can carry a total of 56 passengers, 26 seated and 30 standing. Photo Coventry City Council/William. Hunt

Cllr Jim O'Boyle (Coventry City Council Cabinet Member for Jobs and Regeneration and CWLEP board director visited NP Aerospace to inspect the prototype. He said: "The proposed VLR network is key to our vision for transport here in Coventry. We want our public transport to be efficient, affordable and most importantly environmentally friendly. I believe it's going to revolutionise how we all travel in this city. Coventry led the industrial revolution and now we are leading the green industrial revolution."

In March 2021 the tram was ready to be shown to the people of Coventry. It was carried on the back of a lorry and taken on a tour around the city, stopping at the Co-op building and the Transport Museum to allow the public a closer inspection. It as then moved from NP Aerospace to undertake static testing. In April another step forward was taken with the installation of the world's first Very Light Rail ultra-rapid charging station at the Dudley testing centre. Built by Furrer-Frey this is the first application of the technology to tramways. It has been used in Spain and the Netherlands on electric bus systems. It is anticipated that the tram's battery can be recharged in three minutes wirelessly and autonomously.

At the Very Light Rail National Innovation Centre at Castle Hill, Dudley, the Test Track was laid for trials of the tram. Here the charge station will wirelessly top-up the battery autonomously at scheduled three-minute stops.

The Very Light Rail National Innovation Centre nearing completion in April 2022.

During the development and construction of the tram, work was in hand to apply the same innovation to the track. A company from France, Ingerop Conseil et Ingénierie, was selected to assist in its development, working with engineers at WMG and with Coventry City Council. The concept for the track (called "Trackform") is for it to be supplied in prefabricated sections that will be 250mm thick and clipped together in a similar way that model railway track is constructed. It was specifically designed to minimise adversely affecting existing infrastructures. They will be laid in the tarmac layer of roads, clipped together and will be able to be removed within 90 minutes to enable repairs. The average cost per kilometre for the system is expected to be £10m, which is significantly less than the £35m-£60m per kilometre for conventional systems.

While the project was very much in its early stages, a tentative plan was outlined with the first route being between Coventry Railway Station in the city centre to the University of Warwick. A potential further route links the University with the proposed growth around Whitley. Ultimately the aim would be to connect the city to HS2 Interchange and UK Central. The plan was to have the first route running by 2025.

It was later announced that the University Hospital Coventry and Warwickshire had been chosen for the first destination as it was one of the city's biggest traffic log-jams. Councillor Jim O'Boyle said he hoped the system would work like the London Underground, where there was no timetable and people could hop on and off. He added that the plans for the very light railway were firmly on track with two proposed routes, The routes opening in 2024 would link the University Hospital Coventry and Warwickshire with the railway station and another from the railway station to the University of Warwick and the idea was that the system would later link with the West Midlands Metro. It was also announced that the system would be automated, however, this was tempered by an explanation that the automation would not be driving the tram, but would shadow the driver, who would be in control. There has been no explanation how this would work.

The test track at the Very Light Rail National Innovation Centre at Castle Hill, Dudley was officially opened in May 2021 . Initially it is to be used to test the Coventry VLR prototype vehicle, but the facility is also open to other clients. To mark the occasion Councillor Patrick Harley, leader of Dudley Council and Andy Street, West Midlands Mayor visited the site. Andy Street said "This project puts the West Midlands on the cutting edge of transport innovation and development and shows how collaborative working is delivering for our region. That these vehicles are going to be tested in Dudley to then be used in Coventry is testament to how we've managed to pull the West Midlands together as one in recent years, and I am delighted the WMCA has been able to play its part to help make this happen. Not only is there clear economic benefits to this scheme, but there's major environmental ones as well. VLR is another modern public transport alternative, which means it can help us ease congestion on our roads and bring about cleaner air as we look to tackle the climate emergency and work towards our #WM2041 plan to become a net zero carbon region over the next 20 years."

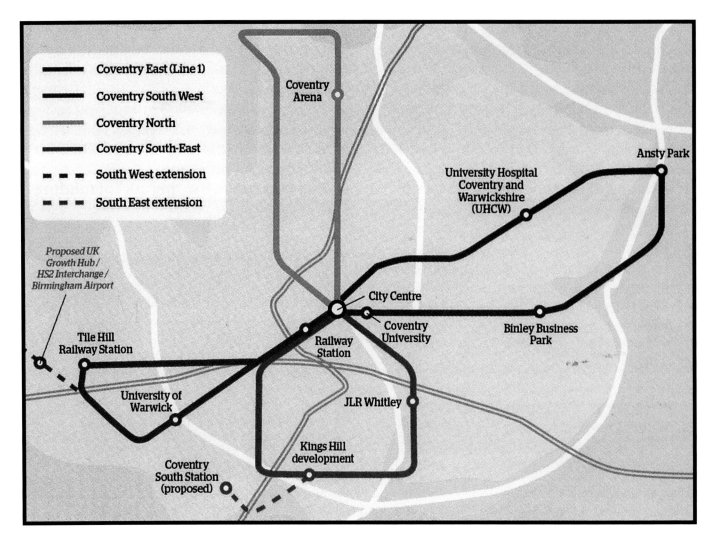

Initial proposals for the Very Light Rail system for Coventry City.

The new centre, sited next to the test track, is due to be completed in 2022 and will have a triple-height engineering hall; research laboratories; conference and seminar rooms; offices for 45 people; public spaces; exhibition areas and an auditorium.

The August 2021 issue of Tramways and Urban Transit contained an article by Nicola Small, Coventry City Council Programme Manager detailing progress of the project. The vehicle was designed by Warwick Manufacturing Group (WMG) and Transport Design International (the latter from Stratford upon Avon) and was due to be tested at the £28M VLR National Innovation Centre, Dudley. She explained that the plan was to use 5G technology to develop the vehicles (called "pods") to run autonomously in a similar way to the automated people mover system at Heathrow Airport Terminal 5. The vehicles will be able to negotiate 15m radii and the trams will be able to "platoon" via a virtual coupling during peak periods, but this could be increased to three vehicles. The vehicles meet the current industry standard of 2.65m wide, so could operate on the West Midlands Metro. The maximum laden axle weight is 4 tonnes. The VLR trams could run on the Metro, though the Metro trams would not run on the VLR tracks. The plan at Dudley is to begin testing remote control operation in early in 2022. At the same time work is currently progressing on devel-oping a modular track system. It is proposed that the track will be preformed in sections around 3m long and 300mm deep. Current guidelines are that all utilities should be buried in the road at least 450mm deep with critical equipment being at least 600mm deep. This will enable the track to be laid over existing utili-ties, giving significant cost savings over standard tramways where utilities have to be moved to avoid hav-ing tram track laid over them. The plan is to build a 1:1 mock up this summer while a 15m long section will be installed at the entrance to Coventry City Council's recycling depot to determine the impact on the track of heavy road vehicles. Coventry City Council has retained ownership of the intellectual property of both track and vehicles so that in future they will be able to earn royalties in future for any use of their intellectu-al property.

In a separate booklet produced by Coventry City Council the Very Light Rail system was promoted . It contained a timetable for the development which identified that the Research and Development phase would be completed in 2022, followed by a Consenting and Planning Phase taking to 2024 and then the Design and Construction of the first section of the first route in 2024/2025.

NP Aerospace were appointed engineers to construct the prototype vehicle. The tramcar was shown to the people of Coventry in March 2021. It was taken on the back of a low loader around the streets of the town and parked up at designated sites for the public to view. The next move was to take the tram to the Dudley Very Light Rail Innovation Centre. However, this was still under construction and the move was scheduled to take place when the centre was completed.

The Light Rail Transit Association had arranged a visit to the Very Light Rail Innovation Centre for members on Friday 22 April 2022 and I was fortunate to join the tour of the site. It was unusual as the building and site were still under construction. As visitors to an active building site we were required to wear boots, visi-vests and safety helmets. While the tour was both interesting and informative, the main building was still under construction and there was only one railed vehicle on site, the battery shunter that was designed to be operated by a worker walking alongside. During our visit the vehicle was stabled in the railway shed and did not move. There were no vehicles under test at that time. Most of the track had been laid around the main building and it disappeared into the tunnel. I did not get the opportunity to find how much additional track there was. I had hoped to see the prototype tramcar built by NP Aerospace and which was due to start testing at the Centre. We were told that the prototype tram is expected to be taken to the centre soon to undertake trials over the 2.2km test track. This is part of the total testing and development stage, expected to last two years, prior to the service trams being built.

A demonstration Very Light Rail line in Coventry has been included in the West Midlands Combined Authority Proposals for its five year "City Regional Sustainable Transport Settlement" (CRSTS) and £54m has been identified to part fund the project.

The pedestrian operated depot shunter. The cover has been opened to show the batteries that power the vehicle.

The bridge carries Castle Hill road and beyond it the entrance to the tunnel can be seen.

Stourbridge Very Light Rail 2006-2022

The railway line between Stourbridge Junction and Stourbridge Town, with a route length of 0.8 miles (1.3km) and a journey time of three minutes, claims to be the shortest branch line in Europe. Built in 1879 its purpose was to enable goods to be carried by rail from the Stourbridge Canal to link with the mainline railway at Stourbridge Junction with a passenger station at Stourbridge Town. Apart from a short break in the First World War it has worked continuously. The branch was listed by Beeching for closure, but re-prieved in 1965. The line was shortened in 1979 at the Town end to make space for a new bus station. By around 1990 the line was single track and operated on the One Train Working staff system. The Sunday service had ceased in order to save costs and in December 2005 this absence allowed the Parry People Mover to be tested by providing a Sunday service. The single unit diesel railcar continued to serve the line from Monday to Saturday.

Parry People Mover PPM50 temporarily parked at the Severn Valley Railway, Kidderminster.

Behind the Class 153 diesel is the shed for the replacement Parry People Movers, with one parked outside.

The Parry People Mover uses a small internal combustion engine to drive a flywheel, which in turn powers the car. The fuel for the engine is LPG and the flywheel also gathers kinetic energy when the vehicle brakes, using this energy when accelerating. In 2008 it was planned to replace the diesel with the Parry People Mover. However, delays in introducing the new vehicle meant that a bus replacement service was introduced until March 2009 when the railcar returned and worked the line until June, when the Parry People Mover took over the service. This change enabled a permanent Sunday service to be reintroduced. The initial car was a PPM 50 unit numbered 999 900 under the TOPS system. London Midlands were successful under the rail franchise scheme and they placed an order for two PPM 60 units. These were numbered in the TOPS system 139 001 and 139 002 and were different from the prototype by being one metre longer than the prototype unit. A depot with workshop was built at Stourbridge Junction Station to house the two units.

In February 2020 the Department for Transport launched a £500 million Restoring Your Railway Fund and invited MPs, local Councils and community groups across England and Wales to submit proposals to use the funds to reinstate axed local services and restore stations. In January 2021 the third and final round of bids was launched. Among the 13 proposals from the West Midlands was a scheme to reinstate the abandoned railway line from Stourbridge Junction to Brierley using the Stourbridge Dasher. The proposal is to run Very Light Rail vehicles similar to the two cars running on the Stourbridge Junction to Stourbridge Town railway. In an answer to a Parliamentary question Chris Heaton-Harris, Minister of State for Depart-ment of Transport, said on 26 July 2021 that an announcement on the outcomes of the bids was expected in the Summer.

In the event the Department of Transport finally decided that it would not fund the application as it decided that the project was more suitable for local funding. However, they did comment that the project was compelling, particularly as 87% of local people were in favour of the proposed service being introduced. Phil Evans, Managing Director at Pre Metro, commented: "We've proved VLR to be the most reliable, frequent, and value for money option for short passenger services – and schemes like ours will truly fulfil the aim of creating accessibility across Dudley. In light of the recent 'Restoring Your Railway' results, we want to let local residents know that the proposed passenger service between Stourbridge and Brierley Hill is still one of our major priorities. We would like to thank the DfT for their consideration and feedback of the project. We also want to thank Stourbridge MP Suzanne Webb for her continued support for the bid and for our existing Stourbridge Shuttle operations. We will now revaluate our funding plans and establish the next steps for this project with feedback from our supporters and local policy makers." Pre-Metro also commented that the project had the support of MPs Suzanne Webb and Mike Wood. It is anticipated that Pre Metro will seek support from the West Midlands Combined Authority to support feasibility studies and establish a business case for the "Dasher".

PPM 50

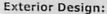

Dimensions:
8.7m long
2.4m wide
3.2m high

Floor Height:
Low 0.45m
High 0.95m (pictured)

Tare (weight):
9.1 tonnes

Seating:
20 without wheelchair
18 with wheelchair
1 wheelchair position
30 standing passengers (total 50 passengers)

Exterior Design:
Option of modern (pictured) or heritage appearance.

Primary Drive Line:
Ford Focus 2L. LPG
1x 12v battery for LPG unit
Through Newage marine gearbox-Tandler bevel box and 4 'V' belt drive to flywheel
2x 12v battery supply for ancillary power
2 LPG bottles with electric change over
Alternative fuel tank with track side supply point optional

Flywheel & Energy Store:
500kg 1m diam normal effective speed range 1000-2600 rpm

Transmission:
Linde hydrostatics through spiral bevel gearbox single axle drive
Second drive axle optional extra

Braking:
Normal braking through transmission (i.e. regenerative) 1m/s^2 (2.3mph/sec)
Emergency braking through sprung on, air off discs at 3m/s^2 with normal adhesion
(Tread and or track brakes available if required)
Air operated sanding gear to the driven wheels

Running Gear:
Solid axle with wheels 610m diam to tram or railway profiles to suit application
Suspension is of chevron type with coil spring optional

Heating:
2 x Water heated air blown

Speed:
25-65km/h (15-40mph) through normal operating range of flywheel

Curves:
15m-radius minimum for standard gauge, smaller radii possible with narrow gauge vehicle

Notice that appeared at Stourbridge Junction Station during the initial trials, informing the public of the technical specification of the prototype Parry People Mover type PPM 50. When the decision was taken to introduce this type of railcar, the two cars purchased were type PPM 60, a metre longer than the prototype vehicle.

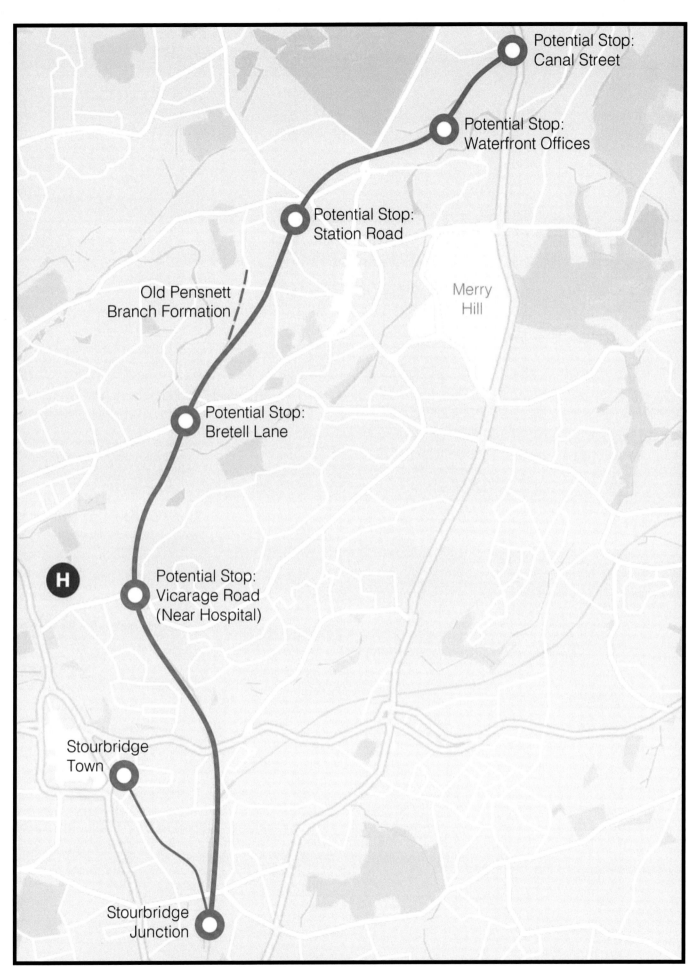

Potential Stop:
Canal Street

Potential Stop:
Waterfront Offices

Potential Stop:
Station Road

Merry
Hill

Old Pensnett
Branch Formation

Potential Stop:
Bretell Lane

H

Potential Stop:
Vicarage Road
(Near Hospital)

Stourbridge
Town

Stourbridge
Junction

Proposed Route for the "Stourbridge Dasher" linking the existing Very Light Rail Stourbridge Town line with Brierley Hill, using the route of existing British Rail freight lines.

The original terminus of the tramway at Snow Hill station. This was closed on 24 October 2015 when the route was diverted to run along the outside of the railway station to Bull Street, later extended to The Library and awaiting the opening of the extension to Edgbaston, due to open December 2021. It is the only West Midlands tram stop to have closed.

CHAPTER 10

Epilogue

When I began writing this history of the West Midlands Metro little did I think I had entered the longest journey I have ever had writing a book. Starting in the autumn of 1999 I fully expected to have the final draft ready to send to my publisher within a year. However, that was without knowing that the world would be thrown into turmoil by a new and virulent pandemic called Coronavirus (Covid 19). The impact on public life was both worldwide and severe. All British public transport was badly affected with passenger numbers dropping by as much as 80%. Governments were forced to provide emergency financial support to prevent the collapse of railway, bus and tram systems. In the West Midlands the Metro was in the middle of a large expansion programme. Work carried on, but with inevitable delays. Large numbers of people were being admitted to hospital and, regrettably, there were many deaths. The public were instructed to isolate at home and limits were placed on trips out. Where possible people were expected to stay at home and schools and colleges were closed. It was anticipated that things would be back to normal after a few weeks. However, the restrictions were not eased until the middle of 2020. But a rise in case numbers led to a return of the restrictions. The pharmaceutical industry worldwide worked on developing vaccines and the first vaccines were approved in December 2020 and a vaccination programme was started in Britain. It was felt that by Christmas things could get easier and the restrictions were eased so that people could celebrate the festival with their families. However, this led to another surge in case numbers and lock down restrictions commenced again in January 2021. In England the full controls started to ease off on 8 March with schoolchildren and students returning to education. However, the stay-at-home requirements for most people remained in force. From 29 March outdoor gatherings of 6 people or 2 households were allowed. People could take part in formally organised outdoor sports and the stay-at-home order ended. From 12 April non-essential retail, personal care premises, libraries and community centres, most outdoor attractions and settings, including zoos, and theme parks could all open. Hospitality venues could open, but serve people outdoors only. The number of mourners attending funerals increased to 30 people, and the numbers able to attend weddings, receptions and commemorative events such as wakes rose to 15 (from 6). From 17 May outdoors, most social contact rules were lifted - although gatherings were limited to 30, outdoor performances such as outdoor cinemas, outdoor theatres and outdoor cinemas reopened, in-doors, the rule of 6 or 2 households applied. Indoor hospitality, entertainment venues such as cinemas and soft play areas, the rest of the accommodation sector, and indoor adult group sports and exercise classes also reopened. Larger performances and sporting events in indoor venues with a capacity of 1,000 people or half-full (whichever was lower) were allowed, as were those in outdoor venues with a capacity of 4000 people or half-full (whichever was lower). In the largest outdoor seated venues where crowds can spread out, up to 10,000 people were able to attend (or a quarter-full, whichever is lower). Up to 30 people can attend weddings, receptions and wakes, as well as funerals. Other life events that were permitted in-cluded bar mitzvahs and christenings. It was announced that from 21 June most other remaining re-strictions could be lifted. However, a new Indian variant had mutated and the stage 4 changes were de-layed until 19 July subject to further delays if required.

Public and staff were required to wear face masks to reduce the risk of spreading the Covid virus. My experience during this time was that the rule was observed by everyone.

April 2021 saw the first delivery of the 21 CAF Urbos 100 tramcars needed for the expansion of the network. Eight were delivered in 2021 and the remaining 13 will be delivered in 2023. All the new trams are equipped for running on either batteries or overhead power. Number 41 was the fourth tram to be delivered having travelled by sea from Spain to Bristol and then by road to Wednesbury. Photo CAF (Compañía Auxiliar de Ferrocarriles S.A.).

Writing this book started in the summer of 2019. The tramway was then twenty years old and no history of the line had been written since John Boynton's book, published a couple of years after the 1999 opening. Being a railway historian at heart, John focussed on the conversion from main line railway to modern tram-way. Since then, the tramway had a relatively quiet life with no expansion for 16 years. In 2015 the tram-way ran in the streets of Birmingham for the first time, when the line was extended outside Snow Hill Sta-tion to Bull Street. Further progress was slow and it was not until 2019 that the trams reached the Central Library. At the same time work was progressing on three other extensions, to Wolverhampton Station, to Brierley Hill, and to Birmingham International station. 2019 was an exciting year for the Tramway and it was time to bring its history up to date. Normally researching and writing a book would take me between six and twelve months. However, that was without taking account of the global impact of the "Covid-19 pandemic". Across the world people were falling seriously ill and dying. Initially there was no vaccine, and it took researchers nearly a year to develop effective vaccines. As detailed above people were confined to home and only essential workers were allowed to travel to work. During the restrictions people were re-quired to wear face masks when in buildings, such as shops, and all non-essential retail outlets were al-lowed to open.

Public transport, including trams, was recognised as essential to enable key staff to get to and from work. Work on the Metro expansions was disrupted with development work first ceasing, then able to continue, but with restrictions. As if this was not enough the discovery of cracks on the chassis of one tram led to the unprecedented withdrawal of all trams while safety checks were undertaken. A brighter light had been seen at the end of 2020 when a national programme of vaccination was implemented, starting with the older members of the public. It took seven months for over 70% of the population to be inoculated. By August 2021 the numbers of people testing positive each day was around 20,000 while hospital admissions were around 5% of people testing positive with 24 deaths per day. The total number of UK deaths linked to Coronavirus by the start of August 2021 had reached 129,743.

In addition to these unexpected events there were other surprises. Whenever I start a book I am never sure where my researches will take me. This book was no exception. It was only after gathering information for almost two years that I discovered the initiatives by Dudley and Coventry Councils, the former setting up a Very Light Rail Research Centre in its town, while Coventry University was promoting and de-veloping a special tramway for small towns, such as Coventry.

On Thursday and Friday, 28 and 29 October test runs were successfully carried out on the newly laid junction and track in Corporation Street and Stephenson Street. It was planned to start driver familiarisation on Friday 31 October. It seemed that the misfortunes happening to the Metro were coming to an end. However, a road vehicle collided with two of the traffic lights at Colmore Circus knocking them down. The resulting damage meant that the tram service had to be terminated at St Chad's stop, while the lights were replaced. The planned driver training had to be postponed.. By Monday trams were back terminating at Bull Street. By 4 November test running on the newly laid track to the Library route was in use for driver familiarisation, without carrying passengers.

In November the tramway service was reduced, with trams being unavailable for service. This culminated on Friday 12 November when just five trams were available for duty, creating very crowded journeys. During the day the tramway published the following announcement:

"We are sorry that there will be no Metro services from Saturday 13 November until further notice. Earlier this year a repair programme was implemented to address cracks identified on several of our trams. As part of this work, it has become necessary for additional repairs to be carried out. To ensure that we can continue to run a safe and reliable service, a decision has been made to remove all 21 trams from service until further notice. This decision has not been taken lightly and we sincerely apologise for any inconvenience that may be caused. Please be assured that every option has been fully considered to avoid suspending the service. As always, the safety of our customers and colleagues is our priority and this will never be compromised. Your patience and understanding is very much appreciated while we work hard to resume services."

The announcement was made in the afternoon of 12 November and the action came as a complete surprise to the traveling public and even some tramway staff were shocked as there had been no warning of the action. This was particularly surprising as after the initial problems with chassis cracks and the cessation of tramway services in June, the trams had been repaired and resumed services. It now seems that the problems were more severe that had originally appeared. It may be coincidence, but the issue has appeared following the fitting of heavy batteries on the roofs of the end units of each tram.

At the Hawthornes stop, Urbos 100 car number 39 picks up passengers on its way to Bull Street.
This was taken on 23 December 2021, nine days after the recommencement of the tram service.

West Midlands Metro announced that the tram service would be halted for at least four weeks while repairs were taking place. The timing was particularly unfortunate as it means that no tram service was available in the very busy weeks leading up to Christmas. The public using the Metro were advised to use alternative public transport, or use the West Midlands Cycle Hire, or walk. Unfortunately, this came at a time when West Midlands Railway informed the public: "Problems reported. Cancellations to services at Birmingham New Street: Due to a member of train crew being unavailable at Birmingham New Street fewer trains are able to run. We're sorry if you've been affected by a cancellation due to a shortage of available drivers recently. This is due to the impact of the coronavirus pandemic on our train crew. Before the pandemic started, we had begun recruiting extra drivers and guards to crew our new trains as part of our plan to develop our service and take into account the higher-than-average number of drivers due to retire around now. Unfortunately, due to Covid-19 and social distancing constraints, our driver training programme has been severely disrupted with over 25,000 training days lost. This has significantly increased the amount of time it takes trainees to become fully qualified train drivers. Training is now being 'accelerated' to bring the train driver numbers up to the full complement".

It transpired that the West Midlands Metro was not the only system to experience problems with cracked chassis. The Inner West Light Rail in Sydney, that also had Urbis 3 trams, had closed their tramway on 5 November, eight days earlier for the same reason. The Sydney system announced that their system could be closed for up to eighteen months. West Midlands anticipated that it could take a similar length of time to repair their trams. However, in the previous few months they had delivery of eight new Urbos 100 trams, which were currently being commissioned. It was felt that these could be used to provide a skeleton service starting mid December. In the meantime there was no tram service in the West Midlands. On Saturday 20 November the Express and Star revealed that the first cracks in the trams had been found not in June, but nearly two years previously, in December 2019. The newspaper also reported that seven trams were repaired and ready to resume duties, however, in order to reopen the services, a minimum of nine trams were required. The West Midlands Combined Authority (WMCA) announced that an independent expert would be appointed to assess the governance of the West Midlands Metro, while the current issues with trams are being examined by the national rail authority.

Car number 42 at the Hawthorns stop also bound for Bull Street.

The public were informed of the closure on the Transport for West Midlands website with an announcement that was not entirely frank about the issue. The announcement stated "Due to the essential maintenance, there is currently no West Midlands Metro service from Saturday 13 November until further notice". It gave details of alternative bus and train services that the public could use. Then it added:

"**Travel Advice:** We are expecting alternative services to be busy, please be patient. Please consider whether your journey is essential and do wear a face covering whilst travelling on public transport and within transport hubs (Unless exempt). If your journey is short, it may be easier to walk or cycle. Or can you work from home?"

The Metro and the Sydney systems were not the only tramways to encounter this problem. There was a similar issue with the three section Urbos trams that operated in Besançon, France. Cracks first appeared in December 2017 in their 19 tram fleet of CAF trams purchased in 2014. Negotiations over the issue were protracted with CAF finally agreeing in 2020 to undertake and pay for the necessary remedial work, which was expected to take two years. It has also been reported that an increase in passenger numbers since the trams were purchased in 2014 led the Besançon Tramway to offer contracts to lengthen each of their current fleet of trams. CAF declined to bid for the order. In addition the internet revealed that cracks have also appeared in CAF trams running in Belgrade, Serbia. The five section trams first entered service in 2011. Unfortunately, it has been difficult to obtain any details of the number of trams affected or the nature of the cracks.

Further concerns were raised when the Australian city of Newcastle, New South Wales, announced on 25 November that their tramway system had been temporarily suspended for at least three days due to an unspecified "mechanical issue". The system opened in 2019 with six CAF Urbos 100 tramcars. The system is catenary-free with tramcars having roof mounted batteries which are recharged at the tram stops. It was announced on 29 November that the issue needing attention was the gearbox. Of the six trams, four required repairs. A temporary service was implemented with trams and buses and it was expected that the repairs would be completed in a few days when the full service would resume by the middle of the week. A spokeswoman said. "This issue has nothing to do with the cracking issue identified in the *(Sydney)* Inner West Light Rail Fleet."

Notices announcing the reopening of the Tramway (though being rather shy about the short working just to Bull Street and not the Library).

The West Midlands Metro service recommenced on Wednesday 15 December with a ten minute service between Wolverhampton St George's and Bull Street using a mixture of repaired Urbos 3 and three of the new Urbos 100 tramcars (numbers 38, 39 and 40). On 18 December number 42 entered service, replacing number 38. After running all day it was on duty again on Sunday 19 December. However, it was removed from operation due to a fault and returned to the depot. It was soon back in service. All tram services ceased on Christmas Day, but were back in operation on Boxing Day and subsequent days with a ten minute service..

Just as the finishing touches were being applied to this book a new error was noticed that in a strange way summarised the history of the Tramway. During the work on the Eastside extension the working area was fenced off in order to keep pedestrians away from the site for their own safety. The fencing carried signs warning the public to keep clear of the area. However, these signs contained spelling errors, which were soon noticed and were highlighted on the internet. They are shown below.

The misspelt signs at the construction of the Eastside extension

To summarise the city centre situation, Broad Street was closed to traffic on 20 January 2020 to enable the construction work to commence on the Edgbaston, West Side extension from the Library. Part of the road was kept open for buses, taxis and service vehicles. As work continued, and the road was excavated to lay track, the whole road from the Library to Five Ways was closed to enable work, including strengthening the canal bridge, to proceed. For considerable periods the whole road surface was dug to enable the tram track to be laid. Fencing was erected along the gutters and special passageways had to be left to enable pedestrians to walk from one side of the road to the other. The plan was that trams would be running a service along the road by November 2021. However, as previously detailed, the problem of cracks in the tramcar chassis emerged in November which meant all thoughts of expanding the service stopped. Indeed the West Midlands was without a tram service until well into December. A truncated service resumed in late December meaning the tramway did not run between Bull Street and the Library. In January 2022 it was announced that the full route to the Library could open by the 30th. However, on 28 January the public were informed that the reopening of the tram service to the Library would be delayed until Sunday 6 February.

At the end of January and beginning of February there was a shortage of tramcars able to be used in service. Indeed, it was announced on 1 February that there would be "delays to the 10 minutes service" and unofficial reports said that at times there were only five trams running the passenger service. Things seem to have got better on 2 February, but clearly there were still problems as on 4 February it was announced that the extension of services to the Library was delayed with no new date given and that the current ten minute service would become a twelve minute service. The Metro also announced that driver training on the Bull Street to Library section would continue, but without being able to carry passengers. A spokesperson said "As soon as we can safely operate services to Library, an announcement will be made"

Broad Street looking towards the city centre. The track is laid, but no trams are running and the opening of this part of the route to Edgbaston is unlikely until April. The overhead-free section from Grand Central will continue along here to Five Ways, where a short overhead will enable batteries to be recharged at the terminus.

On 9 February 2022 the website "Birmingham Live" (part of the Birmingham Mail Group) published an article reminding the public that it was now 200 days since the tramway provided a service between Bull Street and the Library, the service having ceased on Sunday 25 July. Additionally, the countdown clocks at tram stops had ceased working, so intending passengers were not being told when the next tram was due. BirminghamLive reported that West Midlands Metro had told them that 'real progress' meant there was an 'imminent return' of services to Centenary Square (the Library), but added that it would only happen if a 'reliable and sustainable service can be delivered'. BirminghamLive pointed out that the West Midlands Metro had set five target dates to reopen the service between Bull Street and the Library of Birmingham. These dates were October 29 (when the new Corporation Street track was signed off), November 14, December 15, January 30 and February 6.

Following the decision to postpone the 6 February date, the Metro said that they were not setting a new target date. Then on 11 February it was announced that the service to the Library would recommence on 12 February. However, a restricted timetable would operate with a twelve minute service in place of the normal scheduled six minute interval between trams. The Birmingham Mail now pointed out that there had been no tram service between Bull Street and the Library for 203 days. 2021 had been a nightmare year for the Tramway. The combination of Coronavirus restrictions, the shutdown of the Tramway to rectify major repairs to the Urbos 3 trams and the construction of the new junction in Corporation Street had a devastat-ing effect on the tramway. Each one was a major issue that would have strained any tramway. In addition the Tramway was constructing two new lines, one to Brierley Hill, the other to the new HST station and then on to the National Exhibition Centre, Airport and Solihull. Let us hope that the coming years will not be as fraught.

To summarise the city centre situation, Broad Street was closed to traffic on 20 January 2020 to enable the construction work to commence on the Edgbaston, West Side extension from the Library. Part of the road was kept open for buses, taxis and service vehicles. As work continued, and the road was excavated to lay track, the whole road from the Library to Five Ways was closed to enable work, including strengthening the canal bridge, to proceed. For considerable periods the whole road surface was dug to enable the tram track to be laid. Fencing was erected along the gutters and special passageways had to be left to enable pedestrians to walk from one side of the road to the other. The plan was that trams would be run-

Tram number 17, the first of the CAF Urbos3 trams, in Corporation Street on its way to the Library.

ning a service along the road by November 2021. However, as previously detailed, the problem of cracks in the tramcar chassis emerged in November which meant all thoughts of expanding the service stopped. Indeed the West Midlands was without a tram service until well into December. A truncated service re-sumed in late December meaning the Tramway did not run between Bull Street and the Library. In Janu-ary 2022 it was announced that the full route to the Library could open by the 30. However, on 28 Janu-ary the public were informed that the reopening of the tram service to the Library would be delayed until Sunday 6 February.

At the end of January and beginning of February there was a shortage of tramcars able to be used in ser-vice. Indeed, it was announced on 1 February that there would be "delays to the 10 minutes service" and unofficial reports said that at times there were only five trams running the passenger service. Things seem to have got better on 2 February, but clearly there were still problems as on 4 February it was an-nounced that the extension of services to the Library was delayed with no new date given and that the current ten minute service would become a twelve minute service. The Metro also announced that driver training on the Bull Street to Library section would continue, but without being able to carry passengers. A spokesperson said "As soon as we can safely operate services to Library, an announcement will be made"

New tramcar number 36 leaving The Hawthornes stop on its way to Wolverhampton.

Tram number 19 runs alongside Snow Hill Station. The entrance to this section of reserved track has caught out at least one driver who attempted to take his lorry along what looks like an inviting stretch of grass, only to find his vehicle bogged down and needing to be towed out.

Just as I was putting the final touches to the book to send to my publisher came the totally unexpected news that the tramway had shut down again. On Saturday 19 March West Midlands Metro suddenly announced that all services had been cancelled all services for the rest of the day due to "operational reasons".

The service did not resume on the Sunday and on Monday 21 March the Tramway announced that the problem was due to more cracks being found, this time in the bodywork of the tramcars, particularly around the doorways. All services would be cancelled until sufficient trams were serviceable, including the new trams that had been cleared for public service. Learning from he previous experiences of closing the tramway, it was announced that no date would be announced for the recommencement of tram services. Temporary arrangements were put in place to enable passengers with valid season tickets to travel by train or bus without having to pay another fare. This was now the third complete closure of the tramway in nine months. Executive Director of Transport for West Midlands, Anne Shaw said after a meeting with CAF: "The meeting has gone very well. We've got their full co-operation in terms of trying to make sure we've got the trams repaired as fast as possible to get the service back up and running as soon as we can. We're still working through the details but they are becoming a lot clearer now so in a couple of weeks time, I'll be a lot confident of giving further information about when the services will resume. We've had engineers that have come in from Spain and other locations that have been working on similar issues. So we've got quite a lot of people here at the moment training up some local people so they can do this work with CAF. We will have double shifts to do the repairs as quickly as possible. CAF have accepted it is a design fault and they are applying all of those repairs in terms of replacing all of the panels."

To the surprise of the public, tramcars did run on the Edgbaston extension from 4 April when one of the new Urbos 100 trams was used as part of the commissioning process for the new track. However, no pas-sengers were carried and the commissioning was expected to take several months before it was possible to open the line to the public.

Tram number 17 turns from Corporation Street into Bull Street on its way to Wolverhampton.

In talks during April between senior executives from Transport for West Midlands and Spanish based manufacturer CAF to discuss the repair programme, CAF accepted that the problem was the result of a design fault and engineers from Spain and other parts of the world were currently in England working on the 21 affected trams and training British workers how to carry out repairs. A Transport for West Midlands spokesperson said: "We are focused on working with CAF to return a safe, reliable service as soon as possible and are very confident that we'll have the trams up and running for the Commonwealth Games. As previously stated we expect the panel replacement works to take a number of weeks and expect to be in a position to provide a clearer indication of timescales in the next week or so."

The Tramway announced that they were aware that the city was expecting that the Tramway would be in service by the beginning of July for the start of the Commonwealth Games in Birmingham and the sur-rounding area on 28 July 2022. The Midland Metro management were 'very confident' the tram system would be back up and running despite concerns. It emerged Government ministers had been having talks with West Midlands Mayor Andy Street, seeking reassurances that the trams would be back on track when the games began. Transport for West Midlands (TfWM) said they were optimistic that services would be resumed prior to the start of the Games.

In early April the Metro announced that they expected the tram service to resume by the end of May, but without giving a precise date. Then on 27 May it was announced that a restricted service between Wolver-hampton St Georges and Bull Street would commence on Sunday 5 June. However, there was a warning that some trams would be running without being fully wrapped in blue vinyl around the doors. The public were reassured that this would not impact on the safety or performance of the tramcars. Officials also said they were "confident" a fully operational fleet will be ready for the Commonwealth Games in July. The Metro also said it was working with CAF to recruit more engineers to carry out specialist repair work and "with this acceleration we remain very confident that a full service will be in operation in good time ahead of this summer's Commonwealth Games We would once again like to sincerely apologise for the inconvenience the suspension of service has caused" There was a further comment "We, of course, share passengers' frustrations the original timescale provided by CAF to restore a service next week has not been met. Despite assurances that enough trams would be available, they have now informed us this is now not possible until the following week due to further snagging work required before the trams meet the quality standards required for acceptance into service."

Many commuters turned up at tram stops on Monday 6 June to find no trams running nor had any trams run on the day before. It was only on the afternoon of Tuesday 7 June that a notice appeared on the Metro website announcing that the tram service would start on Thursday 9 June, running between Wolverhampton St Georges and Bull Street. This also mentioned that the repaired trams that would be in service would have some plain panels as the blue vinal livery would be applied later.

On Thursday 9 June seven of the eight Urbos 100 tram were seen (the missing tram was number 44) with one Urbos 3, number 22, though the website "BirminghamLive" reported that there was no published time-table although there were 12 trams in service, running every 12 to 15 minutes". However, my experience matched the eight trams recorded on the "British Trams Online" website (published the day the service resumed).

Tramcar number 22 showing three new panels on each side of section 1 and 5.

Sections 2 and 4 each had five new panels on each side.

As heartening as the return to service was there was a less welcome message warning the public that there would be essential maintenance work meaning that there would be no tram service over different parts of the line from 22.00 on various days between Sunday 12 June to Monday 4 July. A replacement bus service would be provided. Because the line continued to be closed between Bull Street and The Library, the Zone 1 fare was reduced by 50p (the fare structure had been changed on 28 March, even though the tramway ceased running on 19 March due to the cracks).

On 10 June the Metro published on its website "WMMServiceUpdate [07:30] Trams are operating every 12 – 15 minutes between Wolverhampton St. Georges and Bull Street. This was followed by a thumbs up picture with the message "Good Service". This prompted two responses, the first from King D saying "12 – 15 minutes is not a good service lol. That's basically Sunday service." This was followed by a message from Andy Randle saying "It's not even a "full" Sunday service until they start running trams across Birmingham (from Bull Street to Centenary Square and beyond.)" The usual weekday service had a tram arriving every six minutes. Surely passengers must feel that this, combined with no service at all beyond Bull Street, is far from a "good service".

On the same day the BBC revealed that the short extension from Wolverhampton St. Georges to the railway station that was due to open by the end of 2021 would be delayed by 18 months "due to hold-ups related to the Covid-19 pandemic."

Tram number 43 was still carrying the "CAF" advertisement it had when being delivered.

It seems that now is a good time as any to draw this history to a close. The past three years have been unexpectedly difficult and the immediate future continues to be somewhat mixed. The Tramway is hoping that the delayed Edgbaston extension will be able to open soon, but the short extension to Wolver-hampton Station has been put back for eighteen months. Construction of the Brierley Hill extension contin-ues and it is due to open in 2023, while the opening date for the initial stage of the Eastside extension has yet to be announced, as the building of the Birmingham branch of the High Speed 2 Railway has been de-layed. The development of the Coventry Very Light Rail is progressing and could point new directions for future Very Light Rail projects, though the Stourbridge to Brierley Hill "Dasher" has gone very quiet.

The mock-up of the design of tram being purchased for the opening of the Tramway. It was dis-played to the public at the depot and in Birmingham and Wolverhampton city centres.

APPENDIX 1

THE WEST MIDLANDS METRO FLEET

Passenger Fleet 1999 – 2015

The original fleet consisted of 16 T69 type tramcars built between 1996 and 1999 by the AnsaldoBreda Company in Italy. The tram body had two sections with a short central articulation. They had three bogies and ran on standard gauge track. The trams had seating for 56 passengers and could take a further 100 standing. Each tram had three 1.25m wide entrances with twin doors. Their length was 24.36m and were the shortest modern articulated tramcars in Britain. There was a rumour that they were originally intended to have three sections and four bogies, but I have not been able to substantiate that. The tram design was unique to the West Midlands. Indeed there were comments on the internet the fleet consisted of 16 trams each with slight differences in the construction, sufficient to prevent a comprehensive interchange of parts. This had an adverse impact on the maintenance and repair of the trams.

The named trams (including the "unofficial" Ernie) all carried four cast metal nameplates screwed to the sides of both ends of the tram.

The last T69 tram to be withdrawn was number 16 in 2015. The trams were stored at Long Marston while a buyer was sought. However, there were no takers and thirteen of the trams were advertised in early 2018 for scrap on Ebay. They were purchased by Booth's, a scrap merchant in Rotherham for £12,000 the lot.

The First Fleet in Service 1999; withdrawn 2006 to 2015; scrapped 2018.

Number	Name	Final Livery	Disposal
01	Sir Frank Whittle*	Red, Blue, Grey	Withdrawn 2006, Scrapped 2018
02		Red, Blue, Grey	Withdrawn 2009, Scrapped 2018
03	Ray Lewis	Red, Blue, Grey	Withdrawn 2013, Scrapped 2018
04	Sir Frank Whittle*	Red, Blue, Grey	Withdrawn 2016, Scrapped 2018
05	Sister Dora**	Magenta, Silver	Withdrawn 2015, Scrapped 2018
06	Alan Garner	Red, Blue, Grey	Withdrawn 2015, Scrapped 2018
07	Billy Wright	Magenta, Silver	Withdrawn 2014, Preserved by UK Tram
08	Joseph Chamberlain	Red, Blue, Grey	Withdrawn 2016, Scrapped 2018
09	Jeff Astle	Magenta, Silver	Withdrawn 2016, Scrapped 2018
10	John Stanley Webb	Magenta, Silver	Withdrawn 2016, In storage
11	Theresa Stewart	Blue, White	Withdrawn 2016, Preserved by City of Birmingham
12	Ernie***	Red, Blue, Grey	Withdrawn 2016, Scrapped 2018
13	Anthony Nolan	Red, Blue, Grey	Withdrawn 2014, Scrapped 2018
14	Jim Eames	Red, Blue, Grey	Withdrawn 2014, Scrapped 2018
15	Agenoria****	Red, Blue, Grey	Withdrawn 2014, Scrapped 2018
16	Gerwyn John*****	Red, Blue, Grey	Withdrawn 2019, In storage

*   Tram 01 was named Sir Frank Whittle in 2005. When 01 was withdrawn in 2006 the name was transferred to tram 04.
**   The nameplate from "Sister Dora" is in the collection of the Chasewater Railway Museum.
***   Tram number 12 unofficially carried the nameplate "Ernie" for one week.
****   The nameplate "Agenoria" was donated to the Chasewater Railway Museum.
*****   The nameplate "Gerwyn John" has been incorporated into a headboard for the Western Diesel at the Seven Valley Railway. In 2016 number 16 became a works car as depot shunter, but it joined the cars at Long Marston in 2018. However, it was not sold as scrap and as far as is known remains in storage.

The surplus first generation West Midlands Metro trams in storage at Long Marston on 23 June 2016, while waiting to be sold. Photo Roger Monk.

Car 10, showing signs of rust, awaiting its fate at Long Marston on 20 June 2019. At the RailLive show it had been used by British Transport Police to demonstrate scenarios involving terrorists and protestors.

Car 05, with its "Sister Dora" nameplate re-moved, sits among re-dundant London Under-ground rolling stock at Long Marston on 23 June 2016. Photo Roger Monk.

Passenger Fleet 2014 – DATE

The specification of the original fleet of T69 tramcars had a limit on the gradient of an incline that the cars could negotiate. The extension along Pinfold Street was steeper than the T69 trams specification. Given the problems the tramway had with these cars it was likely that this inability was a welcome reason to purchase new trams. After inviting bids, the chosen manufacturer was CAF (Compañía Auxiliar de Ferrocarriles S.A.) and the tramcars their Urbos 3 design.

The Second Fleet in Service 2014/15.

Number	Name	1st Livery	2nd Livery	3rd Livery
17		White, Grey, Pink	Blue, Silver, Black	
18		White, Grey, Pink	White, Blue, Silver	Blue, Silver, Black
19		White, Grey, Pink	White, Blue, Silver	Blue, Silver, Black
20		White, Grey, Pink	Blue, Silver, Black	
21		White, Grey, Pink	White, Blue, Silver	Blue, Silver, Black
22		White, Grey, Pink	Blue, Silver, Black	
23		White, Grey, Pink	Blue, Silver, Black	
24		White, Grey, Pink	Blue, Silver, Black	
25		White, Grey, Pink	Blue, Silver, Black	
26		White, Grey, Pink	Blue, Silver, Black	
27		White, Grey, Pink	Blue, Silver, Black	
28	Jasper Carrott	White, Grey, Pink	Blue, Silver, Black	
29		White, Grey, Pink	Blue, Silver, Black	
30		White, Grey, Pink	Blue, Silver, Black	
31	Cyrille Regis MBE	White, Grey, Pink	Blue, Silver, Black	
32		White, Grey, Pink	Blue, Silver, Black	
33		White, Grey, Pink	Blue, Silver, Black	
34		White, Grey, Pink	Blue, Silver, Black	
35	Angus Adams*	White, Grey, Pink	Blue, Silver, Black	
36		White, Grey, Pink	White, Blue, Silver	Blue, Silver, Black
37	Ozzy Osbourne	White, Grey, Pink	Blue, Silver, Black	

* Number 35 had been named "Angus Adams" by the Queen on the 19 November 2015, but no longer carries the name.

For Christmas 2019 nine tramcars were temporarily given reindeer names:

17 – Dancer	20 – Prancer	22 – Dasher
23 – Comet	26 – Donner	29 – Cupid
33 – Vixen	34 – Blitzen	36 – Rudolph

Like all the names on the CAF Urbos 3 tramcars the names of Santa's reindeers were printed on self-adhesive vinyl. Trams were given the names of Santa's reindeer in December 2019 for the Christmas and the New Year celebrations. The Metro ran a competition to spot all nine and send-ing the list to Metro. The prize was a family ticket to the National Sea Life Centre, Birmingham.

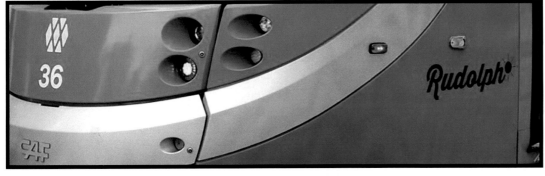

Car 36 was chosen to carry the name "Rudolf" for the Christmas period.

Tram 31 is named after the late Cyrille Regis , a football player who was a member of many teams in his career, including West Bromwich Albion, Coventry and England. Uniquely the name is carried above the windows and includes a silhouette of him.

In October 2019 the West Midlands Metro ordered a further 21 new Urbos trams from CAF to meet the needs of the expanding network. The first eight were delivered in 2021, the remaining thirteen are due to be delivered by 2023. The first tramcar arrived on 28 April 2021 and unexpectedly was number 39. The design of the new trams has been identified as Urbos 100, as the design is slightly different from the previous West Midlands Metro trams designated Urbos 3.

Number	Name	Livery	Delivered	In Service
38		Blue, Silver, Black	09-06-2021	15-12-2021
39		Blue, Silver, Black	28-04-2021	15-12-2021
40		Blue, Silver, Black	26-05-2021	15-12-2021
41		Blue, Silver, Black	23-06-2021	18-03-2022
42		Blue, Silver, Black	14-07-2021	18-12-2021
43		Blue, Silver, Black	24-07-2021	07-06-2022
44		Blue, Silver, Black	06-10-2021	10-06-2022
45		Blue, Silver, Black	10-11-2021	13-01-2022
46				
47				
48				
49				
50				
51				
52				
53				
54				
55				
56				
57				
58				

LIVERIES

In common with other public transport vehicles, the livery of a modern tramcar is not painted. They have a pre-coloured and printed, self-adhesive vinyl covering. The Metro, unlike many other tramways, does not offer full, all-over advertising, although some of the Urbos 3 tramcars have had an advertisement that is both roof mounted and covers the whole of the centre section of the car. This includes contra-vision over the side windows of the centre section. This is said to show the advertisement from the outside but allow passengers in the car to see out. In my experience passengers dislike these as they cannot see clearly which tram stop the car is at.

The details below give the first year a change of livery was first seen. It takes many months for the new livery to be applied to the whole fleet, so there is a period when old and new liveries can be seen.

1998 The demonstration mock-up was painted slightly differently each side. Both were yellow, but there was a shade difference between them. Visitors viewing the mock-up were asked to vote which colour they preferred. Before any trams were delivered it was decided to change the livery meaning one tram that had been given the yellow livery had to be repainted.

1998 Left :The demonstration mock-up of the tramcar, showing the originally pro-posed yellow liv-ery that was changed to the blue, red, grey and green before any trams were delivered to the Metro.

1999 When the trams arrived in Britain they were in the red, blue and grey livery.

1999 Right :The chosen livery for the delivered tramcars. Here tram 03 picks up passengers at the St George's tram stop Wolverhampton.

2007 A new livery was introduced, magenta and silver.

2007 Left: Trams numbers 05 and 10 at Wednesbury Parkway stop. Tram 10 is on the track leading to the depot entrance, while 05 is on the mainline to Wolverhampton.

2013 Tram 11 was repainted in the old Birmingham Corporation colours to mark the 60th anniversary of the final tram running in the city.

2013 Right: To celebrate the 60th Anniversary of the closing of Birmingham Corporation Tramways in 2013, tram 11 was given a livery based on the blue and cream colours carried by the Birmingham tramcars from 1904 to 1953.

2014 On 5th September 2014 the first CAF tramcars entered service in a new version of the magenta and silver livery

Right: Tram 24 enters Priest-field tram stop heading for Birmingham. The new tramcars have the magenta and silver livery similar to that carried by the repainted T69 cars.

2018 With the transfer of operator to Transport for West Midlands, a new livery was introduced of all blue with silver outline for the cabs and black frames for the doors. The name of the system was changed to "West Midlands Metro".

Tram 32 in the new blue livery has left Grand Central stop and is in Bull Street on its way to Wolverhampton.

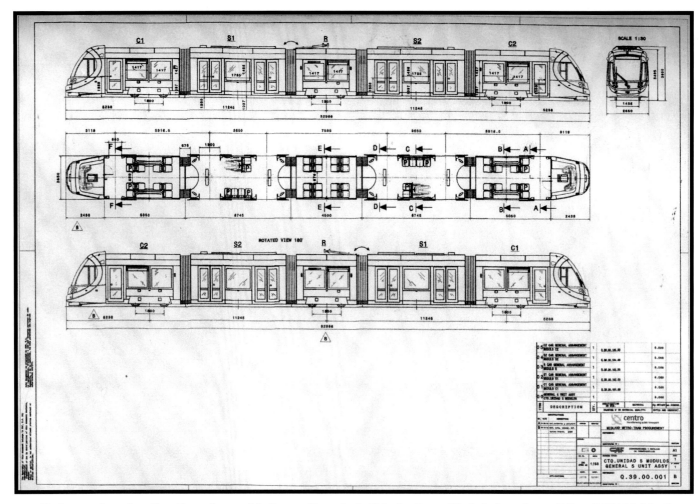

Released under the Freedom of Information Act, this is the official drawing of the CAF Urbis 3 tramcar purchased by the Midland Metro Limited. Drawing Midland Metro Ltd.

2019 To mark the 20th Anniversary of the Tramway cars 18, 19, 21 and 36 were given a special commemorative livery of white, blue and silver. In 2020 the advertisements were replaced by more conventional subjects.

Number 19 outside New Street Station with the full anniversary livery. Photo Elliott Brown (original photo with height slightly trimmed).

Number 21 entering Bull Street from the reserved track alongside Snow Hill Station. It has the anniversary livery now obscured by an overall advertisement for "Just Eat". Photo SV Photog-

Tramcar number 39, one of the eight Urbos 100 trams delivered in late 2021 to enable the fleet to add the Edgbaston and Wolverhampton Station extensions to the main route. Four of them (38, 39, 40 and 42) were commissioned in December 2021 to enable the service between Wolverhampton and Bull Street to be reopened while some of the Urbos 3 trams were being repaired.

The West Midlands Metro road-rail cherry picker registration T977 JPP. Seen fitted with a basket platform on 16 May 2009. Other fitments are available depending on the requirements of the job.

APPENDIX 2

THE WEST MIDLANDS METRO ANCILLARY VEHICLES

It has become the practice for the new generation of British tramways to contract out major refurbishment or developments, while routine maintenance is mainly carried out "in house". Also there is less public interest in the support vehicles on modern tramways and West Midlands Metro is no exception. This has meant that there is not a lot of information on the support vehicles owned by the Metro. However, the Industrial Railway Society (https://irsociety.co.uk/) records them based on reports submitted by members and others. The basic details of the vehicles have been published in their popular series titled "Existing Locomotives Handbook" (available at https://irsshop.co.uk/) Also when work is contracted out the contractors provide their own specialist vehicles. To add a little confusion, contractor's vehicles were often parked in the depot yard among those works vehicles owned by the Tramway. The vehicles detailed below are those vehicles that I am confident are part of the Metro ancillary fleet. A listing of the known contractors' vehicles is given at the end of the Appendix.

LIST OF METRO ANCILLARY VEHICLES

RAIL

Vehicle	Date	Manufacturer	Notes
SET Ltd. RAILCAT robot battery powered shunter	c2007/8	1021/1	**Named ERNIE**
Permaquip scissors platform lift number PL57		------	
Small flat bed wagon EG04	c2008	------	
Hand trolley		------	
Giesmar 4 seat rail trolley	2008	ST/08/03	
Tram T69 number 16		------	Scrapped 2019

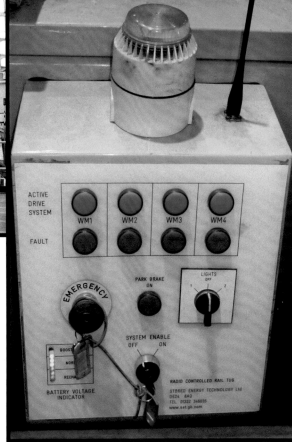

Above: The SET Ltd. (Stored Energy Technology) battery driven depot shunter. It is used to move trams around areas with no overhead power. The "driver" walks alongside when controlling the vehicle using the console on the side of the vehicle or a remote control radio handset.

Right: The shunter is driven by an engineer walking alongside using this control panel. Photo Roger Monk.

Permaquip Scissors lift to enable engineers to access the overhead lines. Seen at Wednesbury on 16 May 2009.

When car 16 was withdrawn from passenger service it was designated the role of works car and parked alongside the depot at Wednesbury. However, this did not last long and it was moved to Long Marston with the other redundant trams.

ROAD/RAIL

Vehicle	Make and Model	Registration Number	Notes
Road/Rail lorry with crane	Hako	BX64 VMA	New 2015
Road/Rail lifting platform	Ausa AT1420	R610 NMJ	
Road/Rail lifting platform	Mecalac 11CX	T977 JPP	Can be used with other attachments
Road/Rail	Unimog	Q179 VOH	
Flatbed three axle lorry	Iveco	R199 EOX	Delivered 5/98; returned to makers 12/09; supplied with snow plough attachment.

Left: Road/rail flat bed lorry with crane BX64 VMA. Photo Kev Adlam.

Mecalac 11CX Road/rail lifting platform with access basket attachment T977 JPP waits in the depot yard on 16th May 2009.

Another road/rail lifting platform. Ausa built R610 NMJ parked in the depot area.

The road-rail Unimog Q179 VOH parked outside the depot building 27 December 2008. Photo Roy Hennefer.

Left: The three axle flatbed lorry R199 EOX rescuing trams 08 and 12 from Snow Hill Station on 22 February 1999 during the test running period. Photo Roger Monk.

Right: The lorry prepares to be attached to the two trams to haul them back to the depot. Note the concrete weight in the rear compartment to aid adhesion and braking when in rail mode. Photo Roger Monk.

Left: The two trams in tow leaving Snow Hill Station and approaching St Paul's stop. Photo Roger Monk.

NON-RAIL (ROAD) VEHICLES AND EQUIPMENT

Vehicle	Registration Number	Notes
Bogie carrier	------	
Box Van	------	
Sandfloh filling vehicle type 102	------	
Sandfloh filling vehicle type 202E	------	

Above: The trolley for moving bogies around when they are removed from trams.

Below: The two "Sandfloh" machines supplied by Mechan for filling the sand boxes

of the tramcars. Photo Mechan.

CONTRACTORS' CONSTRUCTION AND SERVICE VEHICLES USED DURING THE BULDING OF MIDLANDS METRO AND SUBSEQUENTLY

Information from records and observations by Roger Monk, members of the Industrial Railway Society and from the data recorded on the website: https://www.ontrackplant.com/

VEHICLE	RUNNING OR REGISTRATION NUMBER	LIVERY
GRANT RAIL,		
Ruston Hornsby 0-4-0 Diesel Electric locomotive works no 425478 of 1959	GR5087 4	Yellow
Ruston Hornsby 0-4-0 Diesel Electric locomotive works no 421435 of 1958	GR5089 6	Yellow
Fairmont ballast regulator (since scrapped)	GR5108 ?	Yellow
Fairmont tamper	4	Yellow
Plasser and Theurer, Beaver tamper	6	Yellow
Plasser and Theurer, tamper/liner	GR5142	Yellow
Robel type 21 unit with "Hiab" crane and box body	GR5098	Yellow
Donelli unit with "Hiab" crane and 4w flat trailer	GR5105	Yellow
Donelli Single line rail gantries (pair) ('Broad' Gauge double flanged wheels, used to assemble and load track panels)	GR5092	Yellow
Flat wagon for track laying machine	GR5084	Yellow
Ex SR Walrus ballast hopper wagon	??5568?	Yellow
Ex PGA ballast hopper wagon	??5070?	Yellow
Ex PGA ballast hopper wagon	??5075?	Yellow
Ex PGA ballast hopper wagon	?	Yellow
Flat wagon (low height ex LU)	GR5082	Yellow
Flat wagon (low height ex LU)	GR5083	Yellow
Swedish track laying machine 'Amica' (on hire to Grant Rail?)		
RMS LOCOTEC		
Hunslet Engine Co 0-6-0 Diesel Hydraulic locomotive, works no. 7410 of 1976	HO15	Blue
Thomas Hill 0-6-0 Diesel Hydraulic locomotive works no 167v of 1966	167 ICI D3	Grey
QUINTON RAIL TECHNOLOGY CENTRE		
Miniloc Diesel Hydraulic locomotive		Purple and white
OHF ELEC-TRACK LTD		
Mecalac 11CX R/R otp lifting platform		Yellow and White
Mecalac 11CX R/R otp lifting platform	L208 OMP	
Mecalac 11CX R/R otp lifting platform	Q205 FLK	Yellow
Unimog/Mercedes R/R lorry and crane	A855 MUA	Yellow
JONES PLANT HIRE		
R/R otp 1604K excavator Atlas		Yellow
HIREMEE		
Thwaites Road/Rail Three Way Flatbed dump truck and 4 wheel trailer (cable laying etc.)	R435 GMJ	Yellow
Thwaites Road/Rail Dump Truck with bucket	R436 GMJ	Yellow
HYDREX		
Case R/R otp 888 Excavator	G419 DDP	Yellow

VEHICLE	RUNNING OR REGIS-TRATION NUMBER	LIVERY
BRECKNELL WILLIS		
Unimog lorry with crane and lifting platform	Q826 GHG	Blue
Genie Cherry Picker Self Propelled		Blue
R/R 1200 Lorry Unimog	Q62 LDV	Blue
TRANS PLANT		
Procor Flat wagon (low height LU)	RW809	Black
Procor Flat wagon (low height LU)	RW816	Black
Procor Flat wagon (low height LU)	RW822	Black
PIVATE OWNER (?) (REGISTERED BY SNCF)		
Flat (ex-sleeper) wagon normal height	ETR 22 RIV 87	Black
POD-TRAC LTD		
Unimog U1200	Q62 LDV	Yellow
Genie Cherry Picker Self Propelled	?	Blue and Yellow
TXM Plant		
Thwaites R/R "Swivel Skip" Dump truck	P671 NOV	Yellow
GT Railservice		
V Meili R/R VM8000 Thermit welding lorry	E LA2220	Yellow
Keltbray Aspire		
DAF R/R 45LF PRB 10 lorry with platform lift	G51 MBU	Yellow
WHITEHEAD PLANT		
Atlas 1204 R/R otp excavator	R/N P144 (later to Strathspey Railway)	
UNKNOWN		
R/R Bucket dump truck	7	Yellow
Lama R/R Scissors lift platform		Yellow

ABBREVIATIONS

R/R Road/Rail Vehicle
otp On Track Plant
LU London Underground

Between March and December 2015 the Metro hired a Minilok locomotive which was used at Wednesbury Depot. It is believed that the locomotive was hired to assist moving the new CAF cars while they were being delivered and commissioned. This photo was taken at its normal home - Quinton Rail Technology Centre, Long Marston, Warwicks, during the 2018 "Rail Live" show (it was not an exhibit). Photo Roger Monk.

Brecknell Willis Unimog Q62 LDV with Pod-Trak Genie Self Propelled Cherry Picker parked at Snow Hill Station over the weekend of 8/9 April 2006.

A contractor's rolling stock to carry people and equipment. The people carrier is self-propelled and able to haul (or push) a small trailer.

On the approach to Birmingham city centre, one of the smaller contractors' works vehicles, carry-ing a generator trailer that appears to need repairs. Photo Roger Monk.

APPENDIX 3

WEST MIDLANDS METRO

PASSENGER NUMBERS (MILLIONS)
SOURCE DEPARTMENT FOR TRANSPORT STATISTICS

YEAR	PASSENGER NUMBERS MILLIONS	REVENUE (£ MILLIONS)
1999-2000	4.8	2.5
2000-2001	5.4	3.1
2001-2002	4.8	3.9
2002-2003	4.9	5.0
2003-2004	5.1	5.2
2004-2005	5.0	5.4
2005-2006	5.1	5.9
2006-2007	4.9	6.3
2007-2008	4.8	6.3
2008-2009	4.7	6.6
2009-2010	4.7	6.5
2010-2011	4.8	7.0
2011-2012	4.9	7.4
2012-2013	4.8	7.8
2013-2014	4.7	7.9
2014-2015	4.4	7.7
2015-2016	4.8	8.6
2016-2017	6.2	10.3
2017-2018	5.7	9.8
2018-2019*	8.3	10.7
2019-2020*	8.0	11.3
2020-2021*	3.4	5.8

Note

* The West Midlands Metro changed in 2018 when the operation of the Metro was transferred from Altram (a National Express subsidiary) to Midland Metro Limited, a not for profit organisation owned by the West Midlands Combined Authority. The Department for Transport Statistics noted this change and commented that for this reason the figures for 2018-2019 and following years may not be directly comparable with those for previous years. However, the change also coincided with the extensions to the route from Snow Hill Station through Birmingham streets to Centenary Square. 2020 saw the start of the Covid virus and the impact on passenger journeys.

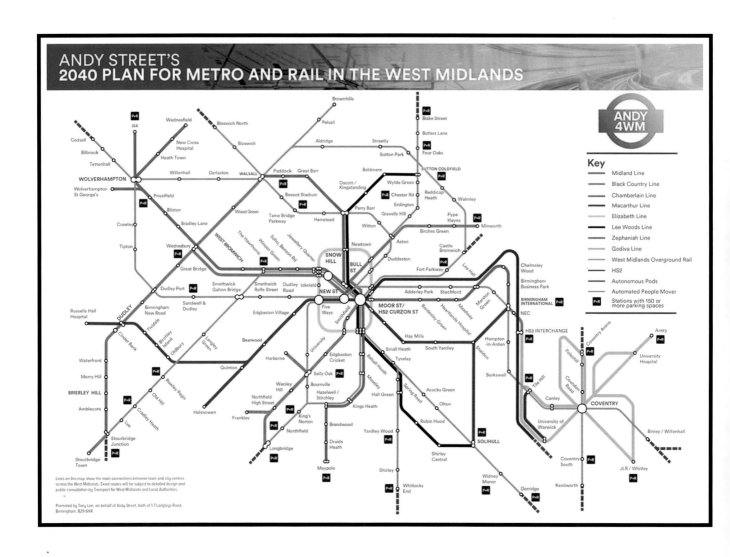

ANDY STREET'S
2040 PLAN FOR METRO AND RAIL IN THE WEST MIDLANDS

APPENDIX 4

Mayor Andy Street's 2040 Vision

EXISTING ROUTES AND UNDER CONSTRCTION

Wolverhampton station to Edgbaston on the map as most of the "Midland Line" the section from New Street Station to Edgbaston is identified as part of the "Macarthur Line".

Wednesbury to Brierley Hill, under construction opening late 2023 on the map as part of the "Black Country Line"

Bull Street to New Canal Street on the map as part of the "Midland Line" to serve HS2 Curzon Street Station.

PROPOSED ROUTES

A Very Light Rail system serving Coventry shown on the map as the "Godiva Line".

Street tramway from Minworth to Longridge to be called the "Chamberlain Line".

An extension of the "Macarthur Line" from Edgbaston to Halesowen.

A Birmingham city centre circle line called the "Elizabeth Line".

A line from Stourbridge Town to Walsall with a branch to Birmingham city centre.

The "Macarthur Line" with two termini in the west of the city at Russell's Hall Hospital and Halesowen and two in the east at Birmingham International Station and Solihull.

The "Lee Wood Line" from Solihull to Sutton Coldfield.

The "Zephaniah Line" from Maypole to HS2 Curzon Street

IN ADDITION THERE ARE PROPOSALS

For an "Autonomous Pod" route from the University of Warwick to Tile Hill

And an "Automated People Mover" from the HS2 Interchange to the NEC and Birmingham International Station.

SOURCES

A Passenger Transport Development Plan for the West Midlands: West Midlands PTE, 1972
Tramways and Urban Transit: News, Worldwide Review and Articles, Issues January 1977 to July 2021
Guided Bus Pilot Project: West Midlands PTE, 1983
Rapid Transit for the West Midlands: West Midlands County Council, 1984
Tracline/6/5 The West Midlands PTE Guided Bus Experiment: West Midlands PTE,1985
Rapid Transit for the West Midlands: West Midlands County Council, 1986
An Introduction to Light Rail Transit in Europe: Ian Dickins for Midland Metro Team West Midlands PTE, 1988
The Metro is Coming: The Times, 1989
West Midlands PTA Report and Accounts 1988-89
Three Year Plan 1989/90-1991/92: West Midlands PTE, 1988
Pack with information sheets promoting tramway, 1998
The Solution to a Growing Problem: West Midlands PTA West Midlands PTE, 1998
Centro Annual Report and Accounts, 1989/90
Midland Metro Parliamentary Bill, 1990
Environmental Impact Statement: WS Atkins Planning Consultants, 1989
Travel Roadrunner West Midlands: Travel West Midlands Staff Magazine, 1990
Centro Bulletin, 1990
Black Country Integrated Transport Study Executive Summary: Black Country Authorities, 1990
Midland Metro Serving the Heart of Birmingham: Centro, 1991
Midland Metro Bill Environmental Statement: West Midlands PTE, 1991
Policy Statement: West Midlands PTA, Centro, 1992
Keeping the West Midlands Moving, A 20 Year Strategy for Public Transport: West Midlands PTA and Centro, 1992
Centro Bulletin; various issues 1992 - 1993
Centro Euro Bulletin, 1992
Midland Metro Bill Chester Road Alignment Environmental Statement Non-technical Summary: WS Atkins Environment, 1992
Midland Metro Bill Chester Road Alignment Environmental Statement: WS Atkins Environment, 1992
Leaflet about proposed Metro: Centro, Altram, 1993
Rapid Transit for the West Midlands Final Report: West Midlands County Council and West Midlands PTE, 1994
Moving With the Times: Centro, 1995
Metro Track Record issue 2, 1996
Low Floor Light Rail Vehicles for Midland Metro: Ansaldo, 1996
The Light Rail Midland Metro Line 1: Ansaldo, 1996
Metro Track Record issues 6 & 8, 1997
Midland Metro Light Rail System: Centro, 1998
West Midlands Transport Package 1998 Volume 1 The Summary: West Midlands Joint Committee, 1998
Metro Update: Transport for West Midlands Metro, 1999
The Metro in the Midlands Issue 1: Centro, 1999
Keeping the West Midlands Moving: Centro, 1999
Transport Update: Centro, 2000
Publicity Booklet Wednesbury to Brierly Hill: Centro, 2000
Publicity Booklet Birmingham City Centre: Centro, 2000
Main Line to Metro: by John Boynton, pub Mid England Books, 2001
An Accessibility Guide: Travel Midland Metro, 2001
Edgbaston Extension Enquiry Proofs of Evidence, 2003
Publicity Booklet Snow Hill to Edgbaston Extension: Centro, 2003
Track Record Issues 4 & 6: Centro, 2003
City Centre to Quinton, Bartley Green, Eastside and Duddeston: Metro, 2003
Towards a World Class Public Transport System: Centro, 2008
Transport in Birmingham England, Birmingham and Fazeley Canal, Midland Metro, M6 Motorway, A47 Road, Birmingham International Airport; LLC Books, 2010
Midland Metro, by Ronald Cohn and Jesse Russell, pub VSD: 2012
An Illustrated History of the Midland Metro T69 Trams; by Andrew Coward, pub Bury Rossendale Rails, 2015
Coventry VLR on Track: by Nicola Small, Tramways and Urban Transit, August 2021

WEB SITES

Birmingham Live: www.birmingham mail.co.uk/whats-on/shopping/corporation-street-is-schizophrenic -doesnt-20943157

British Trams on Line News: www.britishtramsonline.co.uk/news/ 2004 to date

Coventry City Council: https://www.coventry.gov.uk/info/113/regeneration/3152/very_light_rail

Dudley Metropolitan Borough Council: https://www.dudley.gov.uk/news/?tags=Very+light+rail

Furrer+Frey: www.furrerfrey.ch/en.html

Google Maps: www.google.co.uk/maps

Mechan Limited: https://mechan.co.uk

Parry People Movers: www.parrypeoplemoers.com

Revolutionvlr: https://www.revolutiovlr.com

West Midlands Metro: https://www.westmidlandsmetro.com

WMG The University of Warwick: https://warwick.ac.uk/fac/sci/wmg/research/hvmcatapult/research/rail/vlr/